What Doesn't Kill

You Makes You

Stronger

By

JEREMY LOPEZ

What Doesn't Kill You Makes You Stronger

By Dr. Jeremy Lopez

Copyright © 2019

This book is licensed solely for your personal enjoyment only. This book may not be re-sold or given away to other people. If you would like to share this book with another person, please purchase an additional copy for each recipient. If you're reading this book and you did not purchase it or it was not purchased for your use only, please return to your favorite book retailer and purchase your own copy.

All rights reserved. This book is protected under the copyright laws of the United States of America. This book may not be copied or reprinted for commercial gain or profit. The use of short quotations or occasional page copying for personal or group study is permitted and encouraged.

Published by Identity Network

P.O. Box 383213 Birmingham, AL 35238

www.IdentityNetwork.net

ENDORSEMENTS

"You are put on this earth with incredible potential and a divine destiny. This powerful, practical man shows you how to tap into powers you didn't even know you had." – Brian Tracy – Author, *The Power of Self Confidence*

"I found myself savoring the concepts of the Law of Attraction merging with the Law of Creativity until slowly the beautiful truths seeped deeper into my thirsty soul. I am called to be a Creator! My friend, Dr. Jeremy Lopez, has a way of reminding us of our eternal 'I-Am-ness' while putting the tools in our hands to unlock our endless creative potential with the Divine mind. As a musical composer, I'm

excited to explore, with greater understanding, the infinite realm of possibilities as I place fingers on my piano and whisper, 'Let there be!'" – Dony McGuire, Grammy Award winning artist and musical composer

"Jeremy dives deep into the power of consciousness and shows us that we can create a world where the champion within us can shine and how we can manifest our desires to live a life of fulfillment. A must read!" – Greg S. Reid – Forbes and Inc. top rated Keynote Speaker

"I have been privileged to know Jeremy Lopez for many years, as well as sharing the platform with him at a number of conferences. Through this time, I have found him as a man of integrity, commitment, wisdom, and one of the most networked people I have met. Jeremy is an

entrepreneur and a leader of leaders. He has amazing insights into leadership competencies and values. He has a passion to ignite this latent potential within individuals and organizations and provide ongoing development and coaching to bring about competitive advantage and success. I would recommend him as a speaker, coach, mentor, and consultant." – Chris Gaborit – Learning Leader, Training & Outsourcing Entrepreneur

ACKNOWLEDGMENTS

Life can be difficult at times. It's filled with many painful moments and with heartache. But with the pain also come purpose and, if you can learn to see and to recognize it, even greater joy. Even suffering serves a purpose. To all who find themselves walking through tribulation, my prayer for you is that you would keep going. – Jeremy Lopez

CONTENTS

PREFACE

What does it all really mean? "Why do bad things happen to good people?" It's an existential question that has been posed for centuries and day by day we all find ourselves wondering if there's truly a purpose for our moments of hardship and trial. "Why did God allow that to happen?" "What was the purpose of it all?" In moments of pain and moments of trial, it can be so very easy to question not only ourselves but also the very nature of God. Are the tests and trials of life things that we've brought upon ourselves or are they, instead, divinely orchestrated by Heaven in order to bring about some greater good – some desired, intended result? Are there truly lessons that exist in the moments of hardship? If so, what are those lessons and could those lessons have come through some other, less painful means? Can we live without pain, or is pain so intrinsically tied to the human condition that it's impossible to escape it?

Is it true that everything happens for a reason? If so, what exactly is the reason? What does the necessity of hardship reveal about the true nature and the true character of God? Surely a loving and omnipotent Creator, in His infinite wisdom, could find a way to reveal greater truths without allowing His children to undergo hardship, right? The idea that the greatest lessons of life can often only be revealed through the greatest moments of hardship in some way makes the Creator seem quite sadistic. Does He take joy in our pain and suffering, knowing that through our pain we are being made stronger? As I began to ponder these age-old questions, I found myself reminded all the more that, though the great mystery of faith can at times seem like an anathema to us, my greatest blessings have always been tied to my most difficult moments.

When I began to feel the inspiration for this book, I began to find myself questioning the years of religious tradition that have for so long defined the way the modern church views the concept of "hardship." Jesus himself said that within the world there would be tribulation; however, it seems that today, as never before, any talk of hardship is automatically equated to an "attack" of the enemy – a roaring lion set to destroy the lives of believers and cause disruptions. And as a result of religious lies, we've become lazy, it seems. We want the easy way out, choosing to believe that the life of the believer is one of comfort, abounding blessing, and very little if any pain. According to the text of the ancient scriptures, though, such is simply not the case, nor has it ever been.

What if I were to tell you that hardship is a part of life itself and that it is the will of God for you to sometimes hurt? Would such a statement seem contradictory to the faith? Would you consider such a statement to be untrue, believing instead that life within the Kingdom is one devoid of struggle? What if moments of hardship are not simply some attack from some enemy dead-set on destroying you but are, rather, a natural part of life within the Kingdom of God? Would that change that way that you viewed your faith? Would that change the way that you view life itself? As I began to ponder the meaning behind "suffering," I found myself beginning to think of the many moments of pain and trauma that we all face within our lives –

those moments that can cut us to the core of who we are and can only be described as a "Living Hell." I couldn't help but find myself wondering, "Why does it happen?" "Why is it even needed?"

This book represents what I truly feel to be one of the most candid, most personal depictions of the process we call "pain." As we journey together throughout the pages of this book, my sincere prayer for you is that you would come away with a newfound sense of optimistic hope and a renewed sense of purpose. Believe it or not, as difficult as it may be to process while walking through the valley of the shadow of death, there truly is a purpose for the pain. You aren't experiencing pain because you're out of the will of God. You aren't encountering pain and moments of suffering because you've somehow "missed it" or have in some way fallen away from the faith. As you will soon see, contrary to the damnable lies of religious tradition, often times faith and pain are synonymous. If you're hurting today, the pain is a reminder to you that you're living – a reminder that you're still able to experience all that life has to offer.

When moments of trial and testing come and when the hardship and pain seem unsurmountable and inescapable, it's often only then that you can begin to tap into your greatest inner, hidden resources. There is a treasure within you that can only be revealed in moments of pain and without pain you will never truly understand the valuable, Heavenly resources at your disposal. As I write these words to you, I find myself reminded of the life of Job. Not only was his pain allowed; his pain was actually sanctioned by the Creator. Although Job wasn't killed, he was hurt in the most shocking, most unimaginable ways. And, as shocking as such a concept may seem for the religious, natural mind to fathom, the pain Job encountered brought great pleasure to God. In the life of Job we find ourselves reminded of what may very well be the most forgotten, most misunderstood truth within the Kingdom of Heaven: "What doesn't kill you makes you stronger."

INTRODUCTION

My father will always be the greatest man I've ever known. Growing up, he was my hero. He remains my hero to this very day, even years after going home to Heaven. Throughout my life and ministry, I've had the privilege of meeting and even ministering with so many of the great generals of the faith. I've shared the platform with literal pioneers of Christianity – men and women who have helped to shape the faith as we know it. For me, though, none of these generals of the faith can even be compared to my father. He was such a man of strong faith and a man of unconditional love. I would have never known the love of God were it not for my father, and without his inspiration within my life, there would be no global outreach of Identity Network today. Needless to say, when he faced illness shortly before returning home to Heaven, I was angry. I questioned. Never let anyone tell you that it isn't okay to question.

How could it have been possible that a man of such great faith could have been allowed to face such illness? The question rocked me to my very core and made me begin to reassess and reanalyze the faith that I had always known. If you were to be truly honest with yourself, you would admit that you have a similar story within your very own life. Like everyone else, you, too, have a story of loss, of pain, and of heartache so deep that it causes you to dread even having to face another day. Chances are you're in such a moment even as you read these words. Also, chances are, like everyone else who has ever walked upon this dusty planet, you also have questions. "Why me?" "Why is this happening?" "What does it all mean?" "Is there some greater purpose?" I want to share something with you here at the very offset that may surprise you. "It's natural to question, but it's even more natural to hurt."

We've become so numbed, so anesthetized to the indoctrination of religion that whenever moments of pain and trial come the most natural, most immediate response seems to be a desire to throw out cheap, religious platitudes, as if such things even have meaning. "I'll be praying for you," we say. "Weeping may endure for the night, but joy comes in the morning." As sincere as we may be and as truthful as such statements may be, these words are meaningless to hurting people – people who find themselves walking through the literal valley of the shadow of death. Let's be honest.

If you're like me, when you're hurting you don't want the pain and agony to be casually dismissed or disregarded. You need the pain to be understood. You need it to be processed somehow, someway.

Sometimes the only answer is "I don't know." "I don't know why this is happening." "I don't know how it ever got to this point." "I don't know why my marriage ended. "I don't know why I lost my job after being there for more than twenty years." "I don't know why she was diagnosed with leukemia even after a lifetime of faithfulness." The questions always abound in moments of pain. But then, in the stillness and in the silence, another, even greater voice seems to speak from within the darkness of the shadows of the valley of turmoil. Though this voice is greater, it speaks in a much more subtle way. It doesn't shout loudly. It simply whispers. It's the inner voice of pain and suffering. This voice says, "There's a reason I'm still here." It gently says, "There's a reason I'm still alive."

When Viktor Frankl wrote the timeless classic *Man's Search for Meaning*, recounting the atrocities surrounding the Second World War, he shared in painful detail how he watched as members of his family died in the Nazi prison camps. In such a time of death, hopelessness, and despair, he noticed that some died simply because they had lost all hope. Others, he said, were able to find a reason to simply make it to just the following morning. Sometimes, in pain, there's a miracle in simply surviving to another day – continuing to live and to experience and to simply continue to feel without giving up. Religion has a way of so casually, so egocentrically dismissing the miracle of survival. Religion says, "You were never meant to simply survive; you were meant to thrive!"

Try telling that to someone who feels they have nothing left to live for, though. The miracle of survival should never be casually disregarded.

If you now find yourself reading these words, you've survived to face another day. And your survival to another day is a very real miracle. Often times, in moments of pain, just making it to another day is a blessing in itself. Others, when facing pain, haven't been as fortunate. This morning, there were some who didn't awaken to greet a new day upon Planet Earth. This morning, there were some who felt they had nothing left to awaken to. Regardless of where you now find yourself, right now, you're in the midst of a process that most of Christianity has seemingly forgotten about. It's a process so very unorthodox that the topic is very rarely if ever even mentioned. You're in the process of suffering.

When suffering comes, she gives no thought of discrimination. All are equal in her eyes. It matters not to her if you identify as a Christian. Your level of success is irrelevant. Your achievements are insignificant. Suffering gives no thought to one's journey of faith or to one's own personal prayer life. Suffering, though, when she comes, arrives as a gift from God – a gift sent from the very halls of Heaven. She comes with a divine assignment – with a Heavenly mandate. How can such a thing be? To even fathom such an idea is boggling to the very tenets of faith we hold dear. When suffering comes, you can't pray her away. You can't cast her out. There is no revival service in which you one can find relief. Your church and your pastor will even seem powerless to help when suffering arrives. There is no prophetic word powerful enough to alleviate suffering's process. She will fulfill her work and will remain present until her task is complete.

Yet, what exactly is her task? To better understand the role of suffering we need only to examine the truth of the process of suffering illustrated within the ancient text of the scriptures. *"The elders which are among you I exhort, who am also an elder, and a witness of the sufferings of Christ, and also a partaker of the glory that shall be revealed: Feed the flock of God which is among you, taking the oversight thereof, not by constraint, but willingly; not for filthy lucre, but of a ready mind; Neither as being lords over God's heritage, but being examples to the flock. And when the chief Shepherd shall appear, ye shall receive a crown of glory that fadeth not away. Likewise, ye younger, submit yourselves unto the elder. Yea, all of you be subject one to another, and be clothed with humility: for God resisteth the proud, and giveth grace to the humble. Humble yourselves therefore under the mighty hand of God, that he may exalt you in due time: Casting all your care upon him; for he careth for you. Be sober, be vigilant; because your adversary the devil, as a roaring lion, walketh about, seeking whom he may devour: Whom resist stedfast in the faith, knowing that the same afflictions are accomplished in your brethren that are in the world. But the God of all grace, who hath called us unto his eternal glory by Christ Jesus, after that ye have suffered a while, make you perfect, stablish, strengthen, settle you. To him be glory and dominion for ever and ever. Amen." (1 Peter 5:1-11 KJV)*

Within this passage of text, we find that the early church did not view suffering the way the modern church does. Suffering, according to the epistle, is described almost as a necessity – as something that not only cannot be escaped but as something to be treasured. According to the text, when suffering comes, there comes also the assurance that the glory of God will soon be revealed. The epistle also seems to denote a certain sense of equality, pointing to the fact that all within the Kingdom will be required to suffer so that the glory of God can be manifested throughout the entire Body of Christ. Recognizing this, then, is it safe to assume that the early church walked in such greater measures of the miraculous and the supernatural because they learned to embrace suffering? Could it be that the early church maintained a greater measure of the glory simply because they had learned to better understand the need for tribulation?

What if the measure of the glory of God, rather than being tied to your prayer life or to your travail, is tied more to your understanding of your sufferings? Imagine that. Such a concept would not only dismantle centuries of religious indoctrination but would also completely obliterate many of the false, erroneous teachings within Christianity regarding the topic of spiritual warfare. Are we meant to always take up arms? When we were birthed into the Kingdom were we meant to always be in the army of the LORD? Was it intended that we always wage war against the unpleasant, painful things – always rebuking, always casting out, and always praying against? If so, this was obviously not the belief of the early church which arose from Jerusalem following the Day of Pentecost. We find also that this was not the belief prevalent throughout the Pauline epistles either.

As you will soon see and begin to realize more and more as you journey through the pages of this book, life within the Kingdom of God isn't always easy. The road ahead will often be treacherous. There will be painful moments – moments that will cut you so very deep that the pain will feel like death itself. Contrary to what the mainstream of Christianity teaches and continues to promote, you won't always be given a "heads-up" of what's coming. You won't always be given a warning of the pain to come. Often times – more times than not – you'll feel completely blindsided when tribulation and suffering come to you. You'll not be expecting it or anticipating it. Tribulation will come to you when you least expect it, and it will cause you to question.

In the questioning, though, will come a greater a more lasting intimacy than you could have ever experienced without suffering. Within the process of the pain, there will come a greater reliance upon the Holy Spirit. When the voice of the Holy Spirit is all you have to cling to, that voice will become all the more real to you. And in the creation of that greater dependence upon the Holy Spirit, suffering will complete her work. And through it all, the glory of God will be revealed and the great treasure within you will be uncovered as never before. There is a process, though. And the purpose of my writing these words to you is that it's time for the Body of Christ to finally grasp the revelation of suffering. If the church is ever to come into a fuller, greater measure of the glory of God, it must first grow up and move away from childish questioning. Rather than dwelling in the realm of self-pity, the church must move into the greater truth that often times life will hurt – and the hurt is the will of God.

Questions serve a purpose and questions in times of suffering are much warranted, in fact. Jesus himself heralded the importance of questioning when he said, "Ask, seek, and knock." The issue, though, is that in times of suffering we all too often ask all the wrong questions – and as a result never mature. The level of your maturity within the Kingdom will always be directly correlated to the questions that you ask. It's time to grow up into maturity in the things of God. Rather than asking "Why did this happen?" it's time to begin to ask, "What is being revealed in me?" Rather than asking, "Why did my loved one die?" it's time to begin to ask, "What am I to learn about the realm of the Holy Spirit?" It simply cannot be stressed enough that though questions are important, the questions one asks should always lead to greater growth and advancement. Without maturity, there will be no glory.

In closing this introduction to you in order to set the tone for the great revelation contained within the pages of this book, allow me to say to you that for far too long you've been lied to. For far too long, rather than being prompted to grow into a greater measure of the fullness of God, you've been conditioned to believe that the journey of faith is a free gift. Here at the very offset of our journey together, allow me to say to you quite emphatically that faith has never been free. Contrary to what your church has told you and what religious orthodoxy has claimed for centuries, there is a price to be paid and it is a very high price. And if you and I are to ever grow into maturity within the Kingdom of God, not only will we pay the price, but it will be demanded of us that we pay full price. There are no discounts. There are no deals. There are no half-price specials. There is only one full price and all who are committed to the cause of Christ will be required to take on the sufferings of Christ within their own bodies – within their own journeys of faith.

When the price is paid, though, not only will there be a greater, more lasting intimacy with the Holy Spirit than ever before, but there will also be revealed a maturity that not everyone within the Kingdom of God has. I share this revelation with you because I want you to prosper. I share it with you because I want you to possess all that God has promised you. And, above all, I share it with you because it is my prayer that you experience the glory of God in its full measure. Unfortunately, within the modern church, we've relegated the grace and the faith of the Kingdom to little more than "bargain-bin" items – things that hold very little value and zero worth to us. "It's free," we're told. "Simply believe," they say. "Jesus has already paid it all," we're told. And yet we say that we desire to be like him. The conformity to the image of Christ cannot come without suffering. And it cannot come without you being required to pay full price, in certain seasons of your life. There is no escaping it. There is no negotiation your way out of it. There are no deals offered. There is no bargaining. There is no way around it. You're going to go through the fires of tribulation.

What we call "hardship" and "struggle" and "tribulation," Heaven simply calls "Life within the Kingdom." Do you truly desire to be like Him? If so, count the cost. You're going to be betrayed. You're going to be mocked. You're going to lose those nearest and dearest to you. You're going to die. But once you join Him in the fellowship of His suffering, you will never lose anything ever again because you will recognize who you truly are. I'm writing this book to you because I want you to know Him as He is – as He truly is. No, the moments of life within the Kingdom will not all be good; but they will lead to good. The moments will not always be only joyous, but they will all lead to a greater joy in the end. I'm determined to know Him as He is. I'm tired of the discounted, half-priced, religious Jesus. I want the real. And I'm determined to pay full price. My prayer and my longing for you, my fellow believer, is that you would desire the same within your own journey of faith.

CHAPTER ONE

OVERCOMING

In the Kingdom of God, it's going to be demanded of you that overcome. In fact, you'll never truly be able to identify yourself as an overcomer without first being required to overcome. Throughout centuries of church history, much has been said about the topic of overcoming – so much so, in fact, that many have been led to erroneously believe that we're born overcomers. It simply isn't true. You're an overcomer when you've learned to overcome obstacle. In fact, even a better understanding of the term is needed within the journey of faith. In order to overcome, you're going to have to first "come over" something – some trial, some obstacle, some hardship, or some moment of opposition. Without developing the tenacity and the perseverance needed to truly overcome and to "come over" the obstacles, you aren't truly an overcomer. Overcomers aren't born, contrary to the teachings of religion; overcomers are made through perseverance. Overcomers are made from people just like you who faced opposition and overcame.

Here at the very offset of our journey together, I want to make it clear to you that Christ will interrupt your life. In fact, the very nature of Christ is a nature of expansion – of forward momentum. You're going to be stretched. You're going to be forced to grow. And with growth will come growing pains – growing pains so intense at times it will feel as though you can't even face another day. Through these pains of growth, though, you are being strengthened. You are being tested. You are being formed and fashioned to more closely resemble the nature of Christ. And when suffering has completed her work in you, you will be made into an instrument and vessel of the Kingdom of God. Until then, though, though you may be a believer, you aren't truly an overcomer. As the Holy Spirit began to impress upon me the revelation that would serve as the basis of this book, it became immediately clear to me that somewhere along the way, because of religion, the Body of Christ has lost sight of the truth regarding the overcoming nature of Christ. Yes, the nature of Christ is an overcoming nature; however, that nature doesn't magically, suddenly become instilled within you. It must be formed and fashioned. It must be developed.

The question begs to be asked, though, where did it all begin to change? At what point did the Body of Christ truly begin to drift away from the truth of the faith regarding the nature of overcoming? When was it exactly that the ecclesia began to depart from the faith once delivered to the saints, as Jude referenced? As I've said for years within my own ministry, prophetically speaking, change doesn't come instantly; change comes gradually as the pendulum of time swings throughout the ages. As generations pass, new revelations begin to emerge and new truths begin to be proclaimed – often times, these new teachings, rather than helping to establish us, serve only to make us weaker. Every revelation shared must be tested and weighed. We find this not only within the writings of the scriptures, as we are admonished to "Ask, seek, and knock," but we find this even as we look back throughout the annals of time to see the great, rich history of the church.

How did the early church view the concept of "tribulation?" Today, in this more modern time, when we think of the term "tribulation," we think of a period of time existing after the "rapture" of the church. Regardless of what you believe about such a concept – whether your eschatological view and theology is that of a literal rapture and a literal, futuristic "end time," let me assure you that the early church established at Jerusalem did not view the term "tribulation" in the way the modern church does. The concept of "tribulation," at least from the perspective of the early, first-century church was in no way a futuristic concept of the end of the world as many now regard it. To better understand this it's important to understand not only the words of Jesus of Nazareth but also the history of the Christian church within the first century. When Jesus spoke to his followers concerning a time tribulation, he wasn't speaking of twenty-first century America, as many claim and teach. No. He was speaking to them, personally.

In the twenty-third and twenty-fourth chapters of the synoptic Gospel of Matthew, Jesus speaks of dire times to come and gives a very direct illustrations of the troubles to come: *"And Jesus went out, and departed from the temple: and his disciples came to him for to shew him the buildings of the temple. And Jesus said unto them, See ye not all these things? verily I say unto you, There shall not be left here one stone upon another, that shall not be thrown down. And as he sat upon the mount of Olives, the disciples came unto him privately, saying, Tell us, when shall these things be? and what shall be the sign of thy coming, and of the end of the world? And Jesus answered and said unto them, Take heed that no man deceive you. For many shall come in my name, saying, I am Christ; and shall deceive many. And ye shall hear of wars and rumours of wars: see that ye be not troubled: for all these things must come to pass, but the end is not yet. For nation shall rise against nation, and kingdom against kingdom: and there shall be famines, and pestilences, and earthquakes, in divers places. All these are the beginning of sorrows. Then shall they deliver you up to be afflicted, and shall kill you: and ye shall be hated of all nations for my name's sake. And then shall many be offended, and shall betray one another, and shall hate one another. And many false prophets shall rise, and shall deceive many. And because iniquity shall abound, the love of many shall wax cold. But he that shall endure unto the end, the same shall be saved. And this gospel of the kingdom shall be preached in all the world for a witness unto all nations; and then shall the end come. When ye therefore shall see the abomination of desolation, spoken of by Daniel the prophet, stand in the holy place, (whoso readeth, let him understand:) Then let them which be in Judaea flee into the mountains: Let him which is on the housetop not come down to take any thing out of his house: Neither let him which is in the field return back to take his clothes. And woe unto them that are with child, and to them that give suck in those days! But pray ye that your flight be not in the winter, neither on the sabbath day: For then shall be great tribulation, such as was not since the beginning of the world to this time, no, nor ever shall be. And except those days should be shortened, there should no flesh be saved: but for the elect's sake those days shall be shortened. Then if any man shall say unto you, Lo, here is Christ, or there; believe it not. For there shall arise false Christs, and false prophets, and shall shew great signs and wonders; insomuch that, if it were possible, they shall deceive the very elect. Behold, I have told you before. Wherefore if they shall say unto you, Behold, he is in the desert; go not forth: behold, he is in the secret chambers; believe it not. For as the lightning cometh out of the east, and shineth even unto the west; so shall also the coming of the Son of man be. For wheresoever the carcase is, there will the eagles be gathered together. Immediately after the tribulation of those days shall the sun be darkened, and the moon shall not give her light, and the stars shall fall from heaven, and the powers of the heavens shall be shaken: And then shall appear the sign of the Son of man in heaven: and then shall all the tribes of the earth mourn, and they shall see the Son of man coming in the clouds of heaven with power and great glory. And he shall send his angels with a great sound of a trumpet, and they shall gather together his elect from the four winds, from one end of heaven to the other. Now learn a parable of the fig tree; When his branch is yet tender, and putteth forth leaves, ye know that summer is nigh: So likewise ye, when ye shall see all these things, know that it is near, even at the doors. Verily I say unto you, This generation shall not pass, till all these things be fulfilled. Heaven and earth shall pass away, but my words shall not pass away. But of that day and hour knoweth no man, no, not the angels of heaven, but my Father only. But as the days of Noah were, so shall also the coming of the Son of man be. For as in the days that were before the flood they were eating and drinking, marrying and giving in marriage, until the day that Noe entered into the ark, And knew not until the flood came, and took them all away; so shall also the coming of the Son of man be. Then shall two be in the field; the one shall be taken, and the other left. Two women shall be grinding at the mill; the one shall be taken, and the other left. Watch therefore: for ye know not what hour your Lord doth come. But know this, that if the goodman of the house had known in what watch the thief would come, he would have*

*watched, and would not have suffered his house
to be broken up. Therefore be ye also ready: for
in such an hour as ye think not the Son of man
cometh. Who then is a faithful and wise servant,
whom his lord hath made ruler over his
household, to give them meat in due season?
Blessed is that servant, whom his lord when he
cometh shall find so doing. Verily I say unto
you, That he shall make him ruler over all his
goods. But and if that evil servant shall say in
his heart, My lord delayeth his coming; And
shall begin to smite his fellowservants, and to
eat and drink with the drunken; The lord of that
servant shall come in a day when he looketh not
for him, and in an hour that he is not aware of,
And shall cut him asunder, and appoint him his
portion with the hypocrites: there shall be
weeping and gnashing of teeth." (Matthew
24:1-51 KJV)*

These apocalyptic statements spoken by Jesus have been the premise for many a frightening prophetic prediction throughout the ages and have been used to market bestselling prophetic books regarding the "end times." It never ceases to amaze me the fear that can be created when one doesn't take the time to study the scriptures. What if I were to tell you that Jesus, when speaking to his disciples, was in no way speaking of future events that even you and I have yet to experience here within the twenty-first century? "World" is a very poor translation within the opening text of the passage. The word in the original language is "aeon," translated as "current age." You see, when the disciples came to Jesus asking what would be the signs of the "end times," they were not asking about the end of the world; rather, they were asking about the end of their own current "age." It is noted in other passages of ancient text that Jesus even alluded that there were some who would not die until they saw all things be fulfilled. Were the predictions of Jesus wrong? Certainly not.

In 70 AD, as the Roman Empire laid siege to the holy city of Jerusalem, the temple was destroyed and literally not one stone was left upon another. The entire city was pillaged and then desolated and finally many portions destroyed. It happened in the lifetimes of the disciples who first heard the utterance. Many of those early disciples were still living when Jerusalem was pillaged. The foreign idols of Rome were brought into the holy city, creating an "abomination." You see, when Jesus spoke to the disciples regarding a time of tribulation, he was speaking emphatically about events that they were to endure within their own lifetimes. And yet, within the teachings, we find a great parallel to our own lives as believers even to this day. Only those who "endure till the end" shall be saved, as Jesus said – only those who will remain strong even in the midst of times of "tribulation."

Even the apocalyptic writings of the Apostle John, while exiled upon the Isle of Patmos reference the destruction of Jerusalem, noting the "Whore of Babylon" which had taken up residence in the Holy Place. Isn't it interesting that within the Book of Revelation there is reference to the 144,000? In the vision, John asks about their identity, and it is revealed that the 144,000 are those who have come out of the "tribulation." Remarkable, though, in the vision we are shown that the City of God is 144,000 cubits – an analogy that those who persevere and overcome tribulation are helping to lay the very foundation of Heaven itself. There's a reason it's going to be demanded of you that you suffer in certain seasons of your life. The reason is because you're being made into the firm foundation which makes up the Kingdom of God upon the Earth.

Unfortunately, the modern church has become so anesthetized into placing all its hopes into the element of escapism. "We'll be rescued before trouble comes." "We'll be able to escape our troubles." "God will never allow us to undergo moments of suffering and tribulation in life." And on and on it goes. The entire time, rather than standing firm through moments of adversity and trial, we've been conditioned to be weak and anemic, devoid of the power to endure. How can you claim to be strong without first being tested and tried? How can you claim to have an overcoming nature without first "coming over" something? As painful and as shocking as it may be to realize, so often within the Kingdom of God, the only way "out" is "through." There are going to be times in life when, as much as you pray, as much as you fast, as much as you spend countless days in travail, you're not going to escape the moments of pain. There will be times when you will not be allowed to escape the times of tribulation within your own life and journey of faith. And, contrary to the damnable lies of religion, this is the very will of God for your life.

Today, in this more modern age of Christendom, we seem to have such a sense of entitlement. "Jesus paid it all," we say – so casually and so flippantly. We seem to think that because the price for salvation has been paid that the gift of faith comes easily now and without a price. "Just believe," we're so often told. Yes, we've become lazy. And we've cheapened the gift of faith, relegating it to little more than some trinket one finds in a bargain bin. Is it truly any wonder why, when moments of trial and tribulation come, so many depart from the faith and question God? Is it any wonder why so many, when the trials of life blindside them and seemingly come out of nowhere, choose to question themselves and question even the existence of God rather than ask, "What is being revealed in me?" My friend, for far too long, you've asked all the wrong questions. Tribulation and moments of trial are simply part of life in the Kingdom of God.

In closing this chapter, I want to share with you encouragement for when you find yourself undergoing trial and tribulation. In the twenty-fourth chapter of Matthew, as the disciples ask about the signs to come, questioning what will be, they ask something else very important: "What shall be the sign of thy coming?" In the original writings, the term used is "Parousia," literally translated "Presence." The disciples, when posing the question, you see, were in no way speaking of some time when Jesus would come again in the clouds. Instead, they were asking when the nature of Christ would be revealed within them. They were asking, quite simply, "When all of these terrible, tragic, deadly things begin to happen, how will we know that you are with us?" You see, rather than asking all the wrong questions, they asked the right questions. Rather than asking, "Why is this happening?" they asked, "What is being revealed in us?" The questions you ask during your moments of tribulation will directly determine your level of maturity within the Kingdom of God. Through the trial and the testing, something is being revealed within you – a greater, fuller measure of the Presence of Christ.

CHAPTER TWO

BROKEN

Have you ever realized within your own journey of faith just how often the scriptures speak of the subject of brokenness? It's truly astounding, really. Psalm 51:17 declares, *"The sacrifices of God are a broken spirit; A broken and a contrite heart, O God, You will not despise."* Psalm 34:18 says, *"The LORD is near to the brokenhearted And saves those who are crushed in spirit."* Psalm 51:8 states, *"Make me to hear joy and gladness, Let the bones which You have broken rejoice."* Notice, though, that in Psalm

51:8, the Psalmist alludes to a truth within the Kingdom of God that is all too often overlooked or so casually dismissed: it's the LORD Himself who breaks the bones. It's the LORD Himself who brings about the brokenness. Such a concept seems to fly in the face of religious teaching and seems to negate so much of what most of Christendom believes about the nature of grace and the gift of faith.

Is it possible that it is actually the LORD Himself who is responsible for the moments of suffering we encounter in life? According to the ancient text of the Holy Scriptures, the answer may surprise you. The answer, in fact, is a resounding yes! Of the many, many innumerable reasons why religion has done such a great injustice to humanity is the fact that it helps to create such a "devil" consciousness. Religion has taught humanity to focus more upon the works of the devil than on the works and the wonders of the LORD. This is why when trial and tribulation come, the first instinct is to question, saying, "It's an attack of the enemy" rather than seeing the pain as part of the process of God. In the loss of a job, it seems it's the enemy stealing away abundance and attacking finances. In the end of a marriage or the loss of a relationship, it seems it's the enemy destroying our happiness. Have you ever stopped to think, though, that even the "enemy" is the tool of God within your life?

What if brokenness is not simply the byproduct of attack but it rather the plan and the purpose of God? Could you imagine such a concept? In fact, wouldn't such a concept completely change the way in which you view the "enemy?" Could it be that Christ is truly LORD of all? Could it be that He truly has made even the enemy His footstool as the scriptures allude? Christianity doesn't believe that, though, instead, choosing to view the enemy as separate from if not equal to God Himself. As a result, there's always some war – always some fight and some battle to be waged. As I've said for years, you were never meant to be in the army all your life, my friend. In fact, to live a life of constant warfare is to dismiss the joys of an abundant life. If you want to truly experience an abundant life within the Kingdom of God, begin to realize that even the moments of brokenness are ordained by God.

Years ago, the LORD revealed something to me that changed not only the way I view the subject of grace but also the topic of faith itself. The revelation isn't an easy one to swallow, though, if you're living within the confines of the religious, natural mind. As you know by now, though, in order for the mind to be truly, fully renewed, the mind must first be challenged – it must be stretched. In order to truly begin to grasp the concept of grace, one must return to the subject of the Potter's House. Yes, you know fully well that you're being molded and being shaped. Yes, you believe that God has a sovereign plan. And, yes, you even believe that all things are being made to work together for your good. But did you know that even the things that we call "bad" serve a purpose also? Did you know that even the "broken" pieces are made to work together for good?

And, yet, the truth of the matter is that the revelation goes even deeper than that. It isn't simply a matter of the "bad" being made to work together for our "good." It's something much, much greater than even that. Allow me to share with you something that you might find rather shocking. It is the LORD Himself who creates the flaws, the broken pieces, and, yes, even what we consider to be the "bad." Allow me to explain. For centuries, much has been said about the Potter's House, alluding to the fact that we are being formed and fashioned upon the wheel of the Potter, in His very own hands. Yet, for centuries, it's been illustrated that we come to the wheel only to be reshaped and molded again. Something's missing, though. That is never what the text states. To better understand this, I invite you to journey with me, again, to the Potter's House.

"The word which came to Jeremiah from the Lord, saying, Arise, and go down to the potter's house, and there I will cause thee to hear my words. Then I went down to the potter's house, and, behold, he wrought a work on the wheels. And the vessel that he made of clay was marred in the hand of the potter: so he made it again another vessel, as seemed good to the potter to make it. Then the word of the Lord came to me, saying, O house of Israel, cannot I do with you as this potter? saith the Lord. Behold, as the

clay is in the potter's hand, so are ye in mine hand, O house of Israel. At what instant I shall speak concerning a nation, and concerning a kingdom, to pluck up, and to pull down, and to destroy it; If that nation, against whom I have pronounced, turn from their evil, I will repent of the evil that I thought to do unto them. And at what instant I shall speak concerning a nation, and concerning a kingdom, to build and to plant it; If it do evil in my sight, that it obey not my voice, then I will repent of the good, wherewith I said I would benefit them. Now therefore go to, speak to the men of Judah, and to the inhabitants of Jerusalem, saying, Thus saith the Lord; Behold, I frame evil against you, and devise a device against you: return ye now every one from his evil way, and make your ways and your doings good. And they said, There is no hope: but we will walk after our own devices, and we will every one do the imagination of his evil heart. Therefore thus saith the Lord; Ask ye now among the heathen, who hath heard such things: the virgin of Israel hath done a very horrible thing. Will a man leave the snow of Lebanon which cometh from the rock of the field? or shall the cold flowing waters that come from another place be forsaken? Because my people hath forgotten me, they have burned incense to vanity, and they have caused them to stumble in their ways from the ancient paths, to walk in paths, in a way not cast up; To make their land desolate, and a perpetual hissing; every one that passeth thereby shall be astonished, and wag his head. I will scatter them as with an east wind before the enemy; I will shew them the back, and not the face, in the day of their calamity. Then said they, Come and let us devise devices against Jeremiah; for the law shall not perish from the priest, nor counsel from the wise, nor the word from the prophet. Come, and let us smite him with the tongue, and let us not give heed to any of his words. Give heed to me, O Lord, and hearken to the voice of them that contend with me. Shall evil be recompensed for good? for they have digged a pit for my soul. Remember that I stood before thee to speak good for them, and to turn away thy wrath from them. Therefore deliver up their children to the famine, and pour out their blood by the force of the sword; and let their wives be bereaved of their children, and be widows; and let their men be put to death; let their young men be slain by the sword in battle. Let a cry be heard from their houses, when thou shalt bring a troop suddenly upon them: for they have digged a pit to take me, and hid snares for my feet. Yet, Lord, thou knowest all their counsel against me to slay me: forgive not their iniquity, neither blot out their sin from thy sight, but let them be overthrown before thee; deal thus with them in the time of thine anger." (Jeremiah 18:1-23 KJV)

Examine again, though, the words of the text concerning the potter's house. Look more closely. Look even deeper. *"The word which came to Jeremiah from the Lord, saying, Arise, and go down to the potter's house, and there I will cause thee to hear my words. Then I went down to the potter's house, and, behold, he wrought a work on the wheels. And the vessel that he made of clay was marred in the hand of the potter: so he made it again another vessel, as seemed good to the potter to make it."* Notice, if you will that the pot was marred not on its own. It wasn't damaged when it came into the potter's house. It was marred in the potter's hand! It was marred BY THE POTTER HIMSELF! It was the potter who marred the vessel, and after he marred it he made it again into another vessel! Oh how I pray that you will receive this powerful revelation, my fellow believer. Once you do never again will you ever question the trials and the tribulations in your life and no longer will you ever blame an enemy for your struggles or hardships.

Brokenness is part of the process of God, as painful as it may be to admit and as difficult as such a concept may be for the natural, religious mind to fathom and begin to comprehend. I know such a teaching goes against centuries of religious teachings regarding the "enemy" and even contradicts generations of teachings regarding spiritual warfare, but the truth is obvious within the scriptures: It is God Himself who breaks us in order to form us all over again! As I write these words to you, I find myself reminded of the teachings of the Apostle Paul who, when he spoke of the power of transformation in his epistles to the early church spoke of moving from "glory" to "glory." Every time the Creator breaks you, He does so only to make you new again – over and over and over again. Yesterday's brokenness has led to today's revelation and, regardless of how you and I feel about it, we have no choice but to be broken again – and again and again – each time being made new.

All throughout life, you and I have been broken by God and in those times of brokenness, it has seemed as though we were facing the onslaught of Hell itself; however, in the midst of the trials and tribulation – in the midst of the suffering – what we have often failed to realize is that it was the hand of the potter, not the enemy, which had been responsible for the breaking process. You brokenness is pleasing to God. You are broken in order to be made new again, and in the process are discovering more and more the need for a greater dependence and reliance upon the voice of the Holy Spirit. When you rebuke your pain and suffering, you are fighting not against an enemy but against God Himself!

As the Holy Spirit began to share with me the powerful revelation of the potter's house, I found myself, first, in a state of shock and disbelief. Again, as I've always said, in order for the mind to be renewed it must first be stretched. Well, my mind was stretched as my old paradigms of religious belief were stripped away. I wondered, "How can such a thing be?" Even more importantly, perhaps, I began to wonder, "Why?" Why would the potter not simply make the vessel into what he desired the first time? If the potter knew the vision for the intended outcome, knowing full well what he wanted to create, why did he mar the vessel in order to make it new all over again? And there in is the power of grace, my fellow believer. The brokenness was his will all along. The marring was his will. He intended it. In other words, to put it more simply and more practically, your pain and suffering was not an accident. It was not some mistake – some moment in time in which the Creator seemingly forgot about you. It was all His own doing, by His very own divine and intelligent design.

And so what does this mean for the life of a believer? Quite simply, it means that you never truly lost your job. You were simply allowed the opportunity to find something even better and more rewarding – something more fulfilling. It means the divorce wasn't the result of an enemy attacking your marriage. No. Instead, it was the hand of the potter forming you into a vessel that could learn responsibility in order to love more fully – in order to depend upon the hand of the potter even more when crafting your own love story. For far, far too long, you've blamed a devil, you've blamed people, you've blamed God and, yes, often times you've even blamed yourself, rather than learning to realize the power of process. In so doing, you've forgotten the power of the sovereignty of God, also, it seems.

But what if the scriptures are really true? What if, as the scriptures declare, it's true that all things work together for good to them that love God and are called according to His purpose? My friend and fellow believer, what if "all" truly means "all?" If "all things" truly means "all things," then there was never any accident. There was never a mistake. There was never some moment moment in which the potter, when crafting the story of your life, exclaimed, "Well, that was a mistake I have to fix." No. It was all orchestrated. It was all divinely purposed. In fact, the purpose *is* the process!

But what if the process and the purpose aren't because of some sadistic nature in the character of God? What if the purpose isn't because God takes delight in suffering but, rather, that God takes delight in the process of reforming you over and over again? What if it is love which guides Him? What if God loves you so much that He wants you to continuously become transformed and molded all over again? And what if, through the process, you are being crafted into a vessel that possesses the ability to understand the process? There can be no true or lasting intimacy with God without the suffering. We love to speak of the concept of divine union in such covenantal ways, expressing how through the good times and the bad we are united with God though our faith. But most often, most never truly believe that. They choose, instead, to seek after only the good and only after those moments that bring bliss and great joy. Such a faith, though fun, is shallow and devoid of substance. In fact, such a faith isn't truly faith at all.

My friend, it simply has to be said that if your faith cannot carry you through difficult times as well as through good times then you aren't truly faithful and you don't truly possess the faith you claim. In closing, I want to invite you to take a journey into the deepest part of the Kingdom – to the place of a more mature understanding. You aren't a victim; you're a product of the processes of God. And the sooner you realize it the better you'll be for it. Can you imagine what would happen if the Body of Christ would finally, once and for all, grow into a greater maturity of faith? Can you imagine the power of the Holy Spirit that would be unleashed within the realm of Earth when the church finally grows up into the things of God and finally, as never before, recognizes the absolute and total sovereignty of God? Oh how Creation is waiting to see such a moment in time. All of Creation is groaning in anticipation waiting to see the Sons of God becoming revealed in the realm of Earth.

In closing, I want to remind you that it has always been the hand of the potter all along – even when it didn't seem like it. And, granted, there were many, many painful moments that absolutely didn't seem like it at the time. But with pain comes growth and fresh perspective. With pain and suffering comes a greater resilience to persevere and to overcome. With pain comes also the understanding of a greater process at work. And when the work is completed, not only will you begin to see that it all served a purpose but that the there was never ever any wasted moment. It all happened for a reason. And it was all made to work together for your good.

CHAPTER THREE

WHEAT AND TARES

I f you were to look back throughout the annals of history, you would find the great pendulum of paradigm's shifting moving back and forth throughout the landscape of the history of the church. With the passing of time comes revelation and greater insight – some beneficial and some not so much. Revelation should always be tested; it should and must always be examined in the light of the scriptures and weighed against the revelations of the past. Yes, God in His infinite wisdom desires to do a new thing within the realm of Earth; however, just because a revelation is considered new in no way makes it healthy or beneficial to the church or to humanity at large. A powerful case-in-point would be "Y2K", one of the many, many great jokes of the Christian religion. It really would be a joke were it not so incredible deadly.

How many times did you hear, as we approached the turn of the millennium, that dire times were approaching and that at midnight the world as we knew it would come to a crashing halt? How many so-called Bible-scholars used the fear and pandemonium to promote their newest book at the time, claiming that the church would suddenly be snatched away into the clouds just before midnight at the turn of the millennium in order to escape the upcoming devastation? Even writing this, I can't decide if the predictions were more in-line with science fiction or comedy. I share this, though, to help illustrate the dangers of certain so-called "revelations" that have appeared within the Body of Christ throughout the ages. Again, every so-called "revelation" should always be tested and weighed against the scriptures.

More than a century ago there was the resurgence of Pentecostalism, as the gifts of the Spirit were ushered again into the church and as the Body of Christ began to discover that the gifts never truly went away to begin with. And then came the great healing revivalists, giving way to the likes of Aimee Semple McPherson, Kathryn Kuhlman, and Oral Roberts. And then came dominion theology and even the latter rain movement, ushering in often strange and bizarre teachings in the Charismatic renewal. And then came warfare – the teaching that every believer has been enlisted in the army of the LORD with a mission to daily wage war against the enemy. As this teaching began to spread, so too did a consciousness which promoted "evil" and the "demonic." Demons were said to have been hiding around every turn, simply waiting to attack believers. Anything "bad" was the result of these attacks, we were led to believe.

I share this to not only illustrate the dangers of certain theologies but, more so, to point out that much of what you believe about pain and suffering has come from faulty teachings and erroneous doctrines of the church. You've been led to believe that rather than going through trials, you're always going to be given some way of escape, if only you'll pray or fast or travail – if only you'll "bind," "rebuke," or "cast out" some devil seeking to attack you. My friend, it simply cannot be said enough that the time has come for you to grow into the maturity of Christ. As the Apostle Paul so perfectly, so brilliantly stated, it's time to put away "childish things" in order to mature into a more proper, more comprehensive understanding of the processes of God.

Through these processes, though, there is taking place, even now, a great separation in our midst – a separation between the wheat and the tares. To put it another way, there is a separation taking place between those who mature into the greater understanding of the things of God and those who will remain content to feast only on the milk of the Word, remaining babes in Christ. In this separation, the more mature and those who have a desire to grow more fully into the things of God are recognizing the vast importance of perseverance. They are recognizing more and more that pain and struggle are natural elements of the Kingdom of God. And rather than asking, "Why me?" they ask, "Why not me?" These more mature believers, as they gain a greater reliance upon the voice of the Holy Spirit, are beginning to realize just how sometimes painful the processes of God can be. And they're determined to go through any storm in order to allow the nature of Christ to be revealed more fully within them.

Before Ruth ever married Boaz and received her promise of redemption, she was required to go to the threshing floor – the place where the wheat was threshed and sifted. This gives us yet another illustration of the importance of threshing – of sifting and of crushing. Allow me to say to you here at the very offset of this chapter that your promise will be found only after you've been sifted – only after you've been crushed. It is on the threshing floor where the wheat is separated – where that which is useful is brought forth and separated from the chaff. Whether you reslize it yet or not, your moments of pain and struggle have served to separate you from the parts of yourself that do not serve you. Through the "threshing" you are being refined and made new all over again. This renewed sense of wholeness, thoughn, cannot come without first the pain of crushing.

"Then Naomi her mother in law said unto her, My daughter, shall I not seek rest for thee, that it may be well with thee? And now is not Boaz of our kindred, with whose maidens thou wast? Behold, he winnoweth barley to night in the threshingfloor. Wash thyself therefore, and anoint thee, and put thy raiment upon thee, and get thee down to the floor: but make not thyself known unto the man, until he shall have done eating and drinking. And it shall be, when he lieth down, that thou shalt mark the place where he shall lie, and thou shalt go in, and uncover his feet, and lay thee down; and he will tell thee what thou shalt do. And she said unto her, All that thou sayest unto me I will do. And she went down unto the floor, and did according to all that her mother in law bade her. And when

Boaz had eaten and drunk, and his heart was merry, he went to lie down at the end of the heap of corn: and she came softly, and uncovered his feet, and laid her down. And it came to pass at midnight, that the man was afraid, and turned himself: and, behold, a woman lay at his feet. And he said, Who art thou? And she answered, I am Ruth thine handmaid: spread therefore thy skirt over thine handmaid; for thou art a near kinsman. And he said, Blessed be thou of the Lord, my daughter: for thou hast shewed more kindness in the latter end than at the beginning, inasmuch as thou followedst not young men, whether poor or rich. And now, my daughter, fear not; I will do to thee all that thou requirest: for all the city of my people doth know that thou art a virtuous woman. And now it is true that I am thy near kinsman: howbeit there is a kinsman nearer than I. Tarry this night, and it shall be in the morning, that if he will perform unto thee the *part of a kinsman, well; let him do the kinsman's part: but if he will not do the part of a kinsman to thee, then will I do the part of a kinsman to thee, as the Lord liveth: lie down until the morning. And she lay at his feet until the morning: and she rose up before one could know another. And he said, Let it not be known that a woman came into the floor. Also he said, Bring the vail that thou hast upon thee, and hold it. And when she held it, he measured six measures of barley, and laid it on her: and she went into the city. And when she came to her mother in law, she said, Who art thou, my daughter? And she told her all that the man had done to her. And she said, These six measures of barley gave he me; for he said to me, Go not empty unto thy mother in law. Then said she, Sit still, my daughter, until thou know how the matter will fall: for the man will not be in rest, until he have finished the thing this day." (Ruth 3:1-18 KJV)*

In the story of Ruth we find great, great symbolism and even a parallel to the words of Jesus – and a parallel even to the power of the Holy Spirit within our lives. Ruth had been given a promise of redemption – a promise that was fulfilled, ironically, on the threshing floor, amidst the crushing of wheat. Jesus, when referring to the Holy Spirit who would come to empower us, spoke of the Spirit in terms of a "Promise." And yet, there is even a more startling parallel here within the text of the scriptures. As we examine the words of Jesus spoken to Peter, we find that there is also an illustration of crushing – of threshing. *"And the Lord said, Simon, Simon, behold, Satan hath desired to have you, that he may sift you as wheat: But I have prayed for thee, that thy faith fail not: and when thou art converted, strengthen thy brethren. And he said unto him, Lord, I am ready to go with thee, both into prison, and to death. And he said, I tell thee,*

Peter, the cock shall not crow this day, before that thou shalt thrice deny that thou knowest me." (Luke 22:31-34 KJV)

Within the passage, we find that "Satan," a word meaning, simply "adversary," desired to "sift" "as wheat." Remarkably, though, it was Peter who stood upon the Day of Pentecost as recounted in the Book of Acts. It was Peter who stood among the other eleven and preached the first Gospel sermon, admonishing all who heard to be baptized in the name of the Lord Jesus. There would never have come such boldness were it not for the sifting. There could never have been a moment of transformation were it not for the crushing – the process by which Peter overcame the "denial" of Christ and also the denial of himself. Today, take heart in knowing that your crushing has always served a purpose and the purpose is not to destroy you but to make you more prepared to answer the call of God upon your life. You will never truly step into your God-given, Heaven-ordained destiny without first being "sifted as wheat." This sifting can only come through moments of crushing. In your most crushing moments of life, you are being made new again.

And yet, even in the midst of the crushing, we find some other transformative process at work – a process so deeply innate that it often goes unnoticed to the natural, naked eyes. When you're pressed, what is within you will always, always be brought forth to the surface. When you're crushed, your true nature will emerge. How interesting it is to note that upon the Day of Pentecost, when the Holy Spirit came upon those faithful believers there was a reference of "new wine." Wine can only come from the pressing of the grape and, as the scriptures make reference; "new wine" cannot be poured into old wine skins. In order for the new wine to flow forth, there must first be a transformation of the vessel. Suffice it to say that if you truly desire for the nature of Christ to be revealed within and through you, there must first come a crushing – a pressing.

"And when the day of Pentecost was fully come, they were all with one accord in one place. And suddenly there came a sound from heaven as of a rushing mighty wind, and it filled all the house where they were sitting. And there appeared unto them cloven tongues like as of fire, and it sat upon each of them. And they were all filled with the Holy Ghost, and began to speak with other tongues, as the Spirit gave them utterance. And there were dwelling at Jerusalem Jews, devout men, out of every nation under heaven. Now when this was noised abroad, the multitude came together, and were confounded, because that every man heard them speak in his own language. And they were all amazed and

marvelled, saying one to another, Behold, are not all these which speak Galilaeans? And how hear we every man in our own tongue, wherein we were born? Parthians, and Medes, and Elamites, and the dwellers in Mesopotamia, and in Judaea, and Cappadocia, in Pontus, and Asia, Phrygia, and Pamphylia, in Egypt, and in the parts of Libya about Cyrene, and strangers of Rome, Jews and proselytes, Cretes and Arabians, we do hear them speak in our tongues the wonderful works of God. And they were all amazed, and were in doubt, saying one to another, What meaneth this? Others mocking said, These men are full of new wine. But Peter, standing up with the eleven, lifted up his voice, and said unto them, Ye men of Judaea, and all ye that dwell at Jerusalem, be this known unto you, and hearken to my words: For these are not drunken, as ye suppose, seeing it is but the third hour of the day. But this is that which was spoken by the prophet Joel; And it shall come to pass in the last days, saith God, I will pour out of my Spirit upon all flesh: and your sons and your daughters shall prophesy, and your young men shall see visions, and your old men shall dream dreams: And on my servants and on my handmaidens I will pour out in those days of my Spirit; and they shall prophesy: And I will shew wonders in heaven above, and signs in the earth beneath; blood, and fire, and vapour of smoke: The sun shall be turned into darkness, and the moon into blood, before the great and notable day of the Lord come: And it shall come to pass, that whosoever shall call on the name of the Lord shall be saved. Ye men of Israel, hear these words; Jesus of Nazareth, a man approved of God among you by miracles and wonders and signs, which God did by him in the midst of you, as ye yourselves also know: Him, being delivered by the determinate counsel and foreknowledge of God, ye have taken, and by wicked hands have crucified and slain: Whom

God hath raised up, having loosed the pains of death: because it was not possible that he should be holden of it. For David speaketh concerning him, I foresaw the Lord always before my face, for he is on my right hand, that I should not be moved: Therefore did my heart rejoice, and my tongue was glad; moreover also my flesh shall rest in hope: Because thou wilt not leave my soul in hell, neither wilt thou suffer thine Holy One to see corruption. Thou hast made known to me the ways of life; thou shalt make me full of joy with thy countenance. Men and brethren, let me freely speak unto you of the patriarch David, that he is both dead and buried, and his sepulchre is with us unto this day. Therefore being a prophet, and knowing that God had sworn with an oath to him, that of the fruit of his loins, according to the flesh, he would raise up Christ to sit on his throne; He seeing this before spake of the resurrection of Christ, that his soul was not left in hell, neither his flesh did see corruption. This Jesus hath God raised up, whereof we all are witnesses. Therefore being by the right hand of God exalted, and having received of the Father the promise of the Holy Ghost, he hath shed forth this, which ye now see and hear. For David is not ascended into the heavens: but he saith himself, The Lord said unto my Lord, Sit thou on my right hand, Until I make thy foes thy footstool. Therefore let all the house of Israel know assuredly, that God hath made the same Jesus, whom ye have crucified, both Lord and Christ. Now when they heard this, they were pricked in their heart, and said unto Peter and to the rest of the apostles, Men and brethren, what shall we do? Then Peter said unto them, Repent, and be baptized every one of you in the name of Jesus Christ for the remission of sins, and ye shall receive the gift of the Holy Ghost. For the promise is unto you, and to your children, and to all that are afar off, even as many as the Lord our God shall call. And with many other words did he testify and exhort, saying, Save yourselves from this untoward generation. Then they that gladly received his word were baptized: and the same day there were added unto them about three thousand souls. And they continued stedfastly in the apostles' doctrine and fellowship, and in breaking of bread, and in prayers. And fear came upon every soul: and many wonders and signs were done by the apostles. And all that believed were together, and had all things common; And sold their possessions and goods, and parted them to all men, as every man had need. And they, continuing daily with one accord in the temple, and breaking bread from house to house, did eat their meat with gladness and singleness of heart, Praising God, and having favour with all the people. And the Lord added to the church daily such as should be saved." (Acts 2:1-47 KJV)

It was only after Peter had been "sifted" that he was able to proclaim the truth of the nature of Christ. Today, as never before within the Body of Christ, there are many who desire revelation, power, and the ability to work miracles; however, no one desires to pay the price – the price of sifting. Jesus, when speaking to Peter, did not say that he would provide escape or even relief from the embarrassment and the agony that would come from his denial. Jesus said, simply, that he would pray for the faith of Peter to remain strong. Do you desire to be used of God to advance the Kingdom within the realm of Earth? Do you desire a greater, more lasting intimacy with the Holy Spirit? This will not and cannot come to you without first an experience upon the threshing floor.

Jesus told Peter that Satan desired to sift him as wheat, and Jesus did not deliver him from his affliction. Instead, Jesus simply said, "I'm going to pray for you." Why? Because there was something in Peter that wanted to deny Christ! Get the denial out of you so that you will be ready to stand and preach with boldness on the Day of Pentecost! When you have been sifted and when all denial of your inner Christ is removed, you will be able to stand with boldness and with confidence. It is only after the sifting that you can truly recognize the gift of Christ that has always, always existed deep within you. Rather than rebuking the sifting process, learn to embrace it with joy.

CHAPTER FOUR

FIRE

The fire serves a purpose, also. *"I am the true vine, and my Father is the husbandman. Every branch in me that beareth not fruit he taketh away: and every branch that beareth fruit, he purgeth it, that it may bring forth more fruit. Now ye are clean through the word which I have spoken unto you. Abide in me, and I in you. As the branch cannot bear fruit of itself, except it abide in the vine; no more can ye, except ye abide in me. I am the vine, ye are the branches: He that abideth in me, and I in him, the same bringeth forth much fruit: for without me ye can do nothing. If a man abide not in me, he is cast forth as a branch, and is withered; and men gather them, and cast them into the fire, and they are burned. If ye abide in me, and my words abide in you, ye shall ask what ye will, and it shall be done unto you. Herein is my Father glorified, that ye bear much fruit; so shall ye be my disciples. As the Father hath loved me, so have I loved you: continue ye in my love. If ye keep my commandments, ye shall abide in my love; even as I have kept my Father's commandments, and abide in his love. These things have I spoken unto you, that my joy might remain in you, and that your joy might be full. This is my commandment, That ye love one another, as I have loved you. Greater love hath no man than this, that a man lay down his life for his friends. Ye are my friends, if ye do whatsoever I command you. Henceforth I call you not servants; for the servant knoweth not what his lord doeth: but I have called you friends; for all things that I have heard of my Father I have made known unto you. Ye have not chosen me, but I have chosen you, and ordained you, that ye should go and bring forth fruit, and that your fruit should remain: that whatsoever ye shall ask of the Father in my name, he may give it you. These things I command you, that ye love one another. If the world hate you, ye know that it hated me before it hated you. If ye were of the world, the world would love his own: but because ye are not of the world, but I have chosen you out of the world, therefore the world hateth you. Remember the word that I said unto you, The servant is not greater than his lord. If they have persecuted me, they will also persecute you; if they have kept my saying, they will keep yours also. But all these things will they do unto you for my name's sake, because they know not him that sent me. If I had not come and spoken unto them, they had not had sin: but now they have no cloak for their sin. He that hateth me hateth my Father also. If I had not done among them the works which none other man did, they had not had sin: but now have they both seen and hated both me and my Father. But this cometh to pass, that the word might be fulfilled that is written in their law, They hated me without a cause. But when the Comforter is come, whom I will send unto you from the Father, even the Spirit of truth, which proceedeth from the Father, he shall testify of me: And ye also shall bear witness, because ye have been with me from the beginning." (John 15:1-27 KJV)*

Throughout the centuries, much has been said regarding the process of refinement through fire. It cleanses. It purges. It purifies. Unfortunately, though, throughout history, where the subject of fire is concerned, the flames of renewal and the heat of refinement have incorrectly been equated to torment, to torture, and, most of all, to divine punishment. If you're ever going to truly mature in the faith and come to a greater understanding of the struggles of your life you're going to have to settle within your mind once and for all that within the Kingdom fire is used not only for power but for purging – and without purging there will be no true or lasting power. What I see all too often within my own life and have witnessed throughout decades of public ministry is that all too often most desire power but never desire the purging. As a result, churches collapse, movements end, men and women drift away from the faith, and reproach and embarrassment are brought upon the Body of Christ. If you truly desire a greater, more unlimited measure of the power it's going to be demanded of you that you undergo unlimited measure of purging and refinement.

I often ask when speaking to fellow believers feeling called to ministry, "How much power do you truly desire?" Most, if not all, always claim to know God in unlimited and abounding measure, desiring to know the Holy Spirit in totality. What the Body of Christ has failed to realize – or has seemingly forgotten, though – is that your power in the Kingdom will forever be directly correlated to the amount of your purging. The two elements – power and purging – are always, always directly related and there is no escaping this principle within the Kingdom of Heaven. In Job, we find reference to this process of refinement, as Job states that through his trials he will come forth "as pure gold." This analogy depicts the pain and the intense heat of refinement – the refining fire of God. It's time to begin to rethink the fires of your life and begin to view the flames not as torment or as torture but as the flames of purging – part of the many, many processes of God to bring about Christ within you.

In the words of Jesus at the beginning of this chapter, taken from the fifteenth chapter of the synoptic Gospel of John, Jesus alludes to the element of productivity within the Kingdom of Heaven. For centuries the passage of text has been used to illustrate "Hell" or some place of eternal torment – some moment where those who are not abiding in the vine are cut off, severed, and cast away. Very little has been said though about Jesus' beginning statements within the passage of text. Notice that even those who *are* abiding in the vine are also purged in order to become even more productive. Those who do not produce fruit are cut off and cast away; however, even those who do produce fruit are purged in order to bring forth even more fruit. And so what are we to make of such a statement? What are we to take away from what at first glance appears to be such an equally ominous statement regarding all of humanity? The text demands that the Body of Christ come to a better, more mature understanding of the symbolism of fire within the Holy Scriptures.

We often fail to realize the importance of the imagery surrounding the account of the Hebrew men who were thrown into the blazing, fiery furnace after refusing to bow to the pagan gods of Babylon. They were not delivered from the fire. They were not delivered from having to experience the fire. They were forced to enter into the flames, and it was only then that the ropes binding them were burned off. Surely, God in His infinite mercies could have dispatched legions of angels to sever the bindings and deliver the believers without them ever even having to be placed into the furnace. However, according to the text, that is not what happened. Not only were the believers forced to enter the furnace, they were forced to enter into the furnace when it had reached its hottest heat - a heat so unimaginably unbearable that even onlookers were overwhelmed by the flames. My friend, never even once have you been given a promise of deliverance from hardship and struggle; you've been given an assurance of an ability to overcome. Yes, there is a very real difference. The only way out is through!

"Nebuchadnezzar the king made an image of gold, whose height was threescore cubits, and the breadth thereof six cubits: he set it up in the plain of Dura, in the province of Babylon. Then Nebuchadnezzar the king sent to gather together the princes, the governors, and the captains, the judges, the treasurers, the counsellors, the sheriffs, and all the rulers of the provinces, to come to the dedication of the image which Nebuchadnezzar the king had set up. Then the

princes, the governors, and captains, the judges, the treasurers, the counsellors, the sheriffs, and all the rulers of the provinces, were gathered together unto the dedication of the image that Nebuchadnezzar the king had set up; and they stood before the image that Nebuchadnezzar had set up. Then an herald cried aloud, To you it is commanded, O people, nations, and languages, That at what time ye hear the sound of the cornet, flute, harp, sackbut, psaltery, dulcimer, and all kinds of musick, ye fall down and worship the golden image that Nebuchadnezzar the king hath set up: And whoso falleth not down and worshippeth shall the same hour be cast into the midst of a burning fiery furnace. Therefore at that time, when all the people heard the sound of the cornet, flute, harp, sackbut, psaltery, and all kinds of musick, all the people, the nations, and the languages, fell down and worshipped the golden image that Nebuchadnezzar the king had set up. Wherefore at that time certain Chaldeans came near, and accused the Jews. They spake and said to the king Nebuchadnezzar, O king, live for ever. Thou, O king, hast made a decree, that every man that shall hear the sound of the cornet, flute, harp, sackbut, psaltery, and dulcimer, and all kinds of musick, shall fall down and worship the golden image: And whoso falleth not down and worshippeth, that he should be cast into the midst of a burning fiery furnace. There are certain Jews whom thou hast set over the affairs of the province of Babylon, Shadrach, Meshach, and Abednego; these men, O king, have not regarded thee: they serve not thy gods, nor worship the golden image which thou hast set up. Then Nebuchadnezzar in his rage and fury commanded to bring Shadrach, Meshach, and Abednego. Then they brought these men before the king. Nebuchadnezzar spake and said unto them, Is it true, O Shadrach, Meshach, and

Abednego, do not ye serve my gods, nor worship the golden image which I have set up? Now if ye be ready that at what time ye hear the sound of the cornet, flute, harp, sackbut, psaltery, and dulcimer, and all kinds of musick, ye fall down and worship the image which I have made; well: but if ye worship not, ye shall be cast the same hour into the midst of a burning fiery furnace; and who is that God that shall deliver you out of my hands? Shadrach, Meshach, and Abednego, answered and said to the king, O Nebuchadnezzar, we are not careful to answer thee in this matter. If it be so, our God whom we serve is able to deliver us from the burning fiery furnace, and he will deliver us out of thine hand, O king. But if not, be it known unto thee, O king, that we will not serve thy gods, nor worship the golden image which thou hast set up. Then was Nebuchadnezzar full of fury, and the form of his visage was changed against Shadrach, Meshach, and Abednego: therefore he spake, and commanded that they should heat the furnace one seven times more than it was wont to be heated. And he commanded the most mighty men that were in his army to bind Shadrach, Meshach, and Abednego, and to cast them into the burning fiery furnace. Then these men were bound in their coats, their hosen, and their hats, and their other garments, and were cast into the midst of the burning fiery furnace. Therefore because the king's commandment was urgent, and the furnace exceeding hot, the flames of the fire slew those men that took up Shadrach, Meshach, and Abednego. And these three men, Shadrach, Meshach, and Abednego, fell down bound into the midst of the burning fiery furnace. Then Nebuchadnezzar the king was astonished, and rose up in haste, and spake, and said unto his counsellors, Did not we cast three men bound into the midst of the fire? They answered and said unto the king, True, O king. He answered and said, Lo, I see four men loose, walking in the midst of the fire, and they have no hurt; and the form of the fourth is like the Son of God. Then Nebuchadnezzar came near to the mouth of the burning fiery furnace, and spake, and said, Shadrach, Meshach, and Abednego, ye servants of the most high God, come forth, and come hither. Then Shadrach, Meshach, and Abednego, came forth of the midst of the fire. And the princes, governors, and captains, and the king's counsellors, being gathered together, saw these men, upon whose bodies the fire had no power, nor was an hair of their head singed, neither were their coats changed, nor the smell of fire had passed on them. Then Nebuchadnezzar spake, and said, Blessed be the God of Shadrach, Meshach, and Abednego, who hath sent his angel, and delivered his servants that trusted in him, and have changed the king's word, and yielded their bodies, that they might not serve nor worship any god, except their own God. Therefore I make a decree, That every people, nation, and language, which speak any thing amiss against the God of Shadrach, Meshach, and Abednego, shall be cut in pieces, and their houses shall be made a dunghill: because there is no other God that can deliver after this sort. Then the king promoted Shadrach, Meshach, and Abednego, in the province of Babylon." (Daniel 3:1-30 KJV)

As we find within the account of the burning, fiery furnace, in the Kingdom of God, even the furnace exists for a very real reason and for a very specific purpose. For far too long, you've been told that you'll never have to go through the flames and through the fires; however, in the Kingdom, though deliverance will always come in the end, you're going to have to go through your moments of adversity in order to see your deliverance. Notice that within the passage of text, it was only when the faithful believers were actually inside the furnace that they became aware of the deliverance awaiting them. Lazy Christianity has taught us for generations that we'll never actually have to enter into the furnaces! It simply isn't true, according to the scriptures, my friend and fellow believer. In order to truly recognize the deliverance provided, you're going to go through the flames.

Your deliverance exists inside the flames of affliction – not before. The deliverance you've been promised is recognized only once you enter into the flames of the furnaces – not before. If you could begin to recognize this within your own life and journey of faith I assure you that you'll never view tribulation in the same way again. Can you imagine the hope that comes in knowing that you're right where you're supposed to be? Think of that for a moment. Rather than questioning "Why?" could you imagine the intense faith that would begin to arise once you gain the revelation that even in the midst of the hottest, most deadly parts of the flames you're still in the very will of God? On how I pray for the Body of Christ and for humanity at large to get this revelation! If you could begin to recognize as never before that in the flames of affliction you're being purged rather than being attacked, never again will you question your God-given, Spirit-inspired destiny within the Kingdom of Heaven.

Right now, as you read these words, chances are you find yourself wondering when deliverance will come. Perhaps, right now, you wonder, "Has God forgotten me?" You find yourself thinking, asking, pondering, "Why me?" And now, all around you, chances are there are other voices saying to you that it's going to get better. Yet, for some reason, it seems to be only getting worse. The debt keeps mounting. The doctor's continue to give a bad report. Rather than looking up, things only seem to be getting a lot darker. Although it may seem that I'm the bearer of bad news, allow me to share with you something that you need to realize and understand: "Chances are it may seem to get worse before it gets better." In other words, chances are the fire will be made hotter. Yes, there's a chance the furnace will be made so incredibly hot that it may seem to be unbearable – even more so than it already seems to be. What I want you to know, though, is that when the furnace is made even hotter and when you find yourself in the midst of the flames, it's then and only then that you will begin to recognize the help existing for you. If it seems your deliverance hasn't come, it's only because the fires haven't gotten hot enough yet.

CHAPTER FIVE

AFFLICTION

When testing comes and when the flames of refinement begin to dance all about you, you will either view the pain and the struggle as an attack against you or, instead, as a divinely crafted process of God meant to awaken the Christ within you and usher you into the next chapter of your destiny. The way that you choose to view the afflictions of life will always directly determine your advancement within the Kingdom. You will not escape struggle and hardship in this life – even Jesus himself said as much. However, you are always given a choice in how you will respond to your moments of adversity. You can either say that you are being singled out and attacked, or you can begin to see that you've been chosen to graduate to another even greater level of maturity in God. The choice, though, in times of affliction, is completely your own.

Perspective is crucial in all aspects of life within the Kingdom of Heaven but never any more so than when encountering affliction. Hear me when I say that the way you choose to view your affliction will determine the maturity you will possess when you overcome – when you "come over" your suffering. My friend and fellow believer, it's time to begin to rethink the meaning behind your struggles and your hardships. God is a God of love and not a God of sadistic humor who takes pleasure in your pain simply for the purpose of His own enjoyment. No. Your pain serves a purpose; it means something. It all means something – much more than we would typically dare to admit, in fact. There's a purpose to your pain.

There's a process at work whenever you are made to suffer for a while. The process, in fact, is a very crucial part of life within the Kingdom of Heaven. You are not only being formed and fashioned through your suffering but are, instead, actually being made into a new creation. There's a reason, you see, why you are undergoing the trials and the testing that you are. In spite of the feeling of devastation, the process of your pain hasn't been a waste of time. It's all been happening for a very real, very specific reason – so that you can be made brand new all over again. You aren't simply being formed; you're being transformed.

I would have been remiss had I not shared with you the revelation concerning the three Hebrews who had suffered the burning, fiery furnace. However, what most may not truly realize is that the incident recounted in the Book of Daniel is not the only time within the scriptures that a fiery furnace is mentioned. We find reference to a burning, fiery furnace also in the prophetic utterances of Isaiah. Only this time, the furnace doesn't belong to a pagan king dead-set on forcing believers to bow to a graven image. No. This time, on the contrary, the burning, fiery furnace belongs to the LORD Himself. In order to understand the true meaning of affliction we need to first understand the, yes, there is a purpose to it. Secondarily, we must understand that the purpose is the process of refinement.

"Hear ye this, O house of Jacob, which are called by the name of Israel, and are come forth out of the waters of Judah, which swear by the name of the Lord, and make mention of the God

of Israel, but not in truth, nor in righteousness. For they call themselves of the holy city, and stay themselves upon the God of Israel; The Lord of hosts is his name. I have declared the former things from the beginning; and they went forth out of my mouth, and I shewed them; I did them suddenly, and they came to pass. Because I knew that thou art obstinate, and thy neck is an iron sinew, and thy brow brass; I have even from the beginning declared it to thee; before it came to pass I shewed it thee: lest thou shouldest say, Mine idol hath done them, and my graven image, and my molten image, hath commanded them. Thou hast heard, see all this; and will not ye declare it? I have shewed thee new things from this time, even hidden things, and thou didst not know them. They are created now, and not from the beginning; even before the day when thou heardest them not; lest thou shouldest say, Behold, I knew them. Yea, thou heardest not; yea, thou knewest not; yea, from that time that thine ear was not opened: for I knew that thou wouldest deal very treacherously, and wast called a transgressor from the womb. For my name's sake will I defer mine anger, and for my praise will I refrain for thee, that I cut thee not off. Behold, I have refined thee, but not with silver; I have chosen thee in the furnace of affliction. For mine own sake, even for mine own sake, will I do it: for how should my name be polluted? and I will not give my glory unto another. Hearken unto me, O Jacob and Israel, my called; I am he; I am the first, I also am the last. Mine hand also hath laid the foundation of the earth, and my right hand hath spanned the heavens: when I call unto them, they stand up together." (Isaiah 48:1-13 KJV)

Within the prophetic utterances spoken by the LORD through the Prophet Isaiah, we find a very startling revelation: that it is the LORD

Himself who is responsible for the furnace of affliction! *"For my name's sake will I defer mine anger, and for my praise will I refrain for thee, that I cut thee not off. Behold, I have refined thee, but not with silver; I have chosen thee in the furnace of affliction. For mine own sake, even for mine own sake, will I do it: for how should my name be polluted? and I will not give my glory unto another."* Notice that the call to the furnace, according to the text, is for the LORD's very own namesake! And notice also that it is within the furnace that the calling is made! Knowing this, how fitting is it to now consider the words of Job who declared that he would come through his trials as "pure gold?"

The glory of God will not be polluted – everything will be burned away through the furnace of affliction until the inner Christ is all that remains. If it feels you can't take any more, then you're in exactly in the right place at the right time. If it feels that you won't be able to make it through your moment of testing and trial, you're exactly where you were destined to be. And if it feels like you're walking through a literal Hell on Earth, keep going because the only way out is through! When the Body of Christ matures to a better understanding of pain and suffering, she will come to an even greater revelation of the hope of her calling.

The LORD, according to the Word of the LORD spoken through the Prophet Isaiah, will not share His glory with anyone. To put it another way, picture, if you will, the process of refinement through which gold is purified. Through blazing, hot, burning fire, the gold is made pure – freed from pollutants. When I began to consider the Word of the LORD and its true meaning, as clearly as I've ever heard the voice of the Holy Spirit within me, I heard the LORD say, "The church has become content with polluted gold!" You see, there's a reason the church worldwide isn't operating in a greater, fuller measure of the glory of God. The reason is because it has failed to realize that the call of the Kingdom demands, at certain times – at certain moments – a call to suffer. Being called to the Kingdom for such a time as this means that in certain seasons of your life you're going to be called so suffer and to endure till the end. It's in the furnace of affliction that the calling is made clear to the believer. And without the affliction the calling is impure – it's contaminated and polluted.

The call of God upon your life can only be recognized through your moments of adversity. Allow me to explain. Sure, yes, you've been given a glimpse of your calling. Perhaps, even as you read these words, you're aware in some way, to some small degree, what you've been called to do for the Kingdom of God. Perhaps, to some degree, there's always existed some burning desire for ministry within your life. But the vision hasn't always seemed clear to you, has it? It hasn't always seemed certain? There have been times, if you were to be honest with yourself, when the calling seemed questionable, at best. And at other times the calling seemed altogether nonexistent. Why? Because, quite simply, although the calling has been placed, the calling hasn't been fully "refined." It's often been a mix – a polluted mix – of what God wants and what you want. You've always had a hunger for ministry; however, you've wanted ministry on your own terms – in your own ways. You've wanted to call the shots.

It's been said for generations that when we are called, we are also equipped. Well, it's true. However, the "equipping" is not what most believe it to be. To be equipped for the Kingdom of God is much more than having gifts and talents imparted and instilled. Equipment within the Kingdom of Heaven is actually, at times, a rather painful, sometimes even devastating process. In order to see the real, the false, the fake, and the temporal must first be burned away through the fires of the furnace of affliction. In order to truly see the heavenly and the eternal, the worldly must first be burned away. You've been entrusted with gold; however, the gold must be refined. The process of refinement will be painful, at times; however, the process is critical if your calling is to ever be truly, fully recognized.

In Leviticus, the sons of Aaron, Nadab and Abihu offered "strange fire" to the LORD. Much has been said of this throughout the ages. The term "strange" within the original text, can be literally translated as "unauthorized." I share this to say to you that far too often, the reason the church has failed to see greater displays of the supernatural is because the church hasn't fully been authorized to access the greater glories and the greater wonders of God. It's wanted to use a glory that has yet to be refined. Rather than seeing suffering as part of the process of God, it, instead, rebukes moments of pain and suffering. It, instead, blames a "devil" rather than giving glory and praise to God. In moments of trial and hardship, it asks, "Why me?" rather than asking, "What are we to learn through this fire?" My friend and fellow believer, I would ask respectfully, has it ever occurred to you that the reason you have yet to experience your breakthrough is quite simply because you have yet to gracefully pay the price you've been asked to pay?

Could it be that in your moments of pain, rather than enduring gracefully, you've always looked for the way out? Could it be that you've failed to see your adversity as one of the many, many processes of God used within the Kingdom to bring about refinement and have instead seen it as some malicious, malevolent attack against you? Could it be, I would ask, that the single greatest reason you've yet to experience the dimension of the greater glories of God is because you've believed the lie that life within the Kingdom is free of hardship and struggle? It's time to shift your perspective away from the damnable lies of religion and begin to see that, no, life will not always be easy and, no, you will not always be given the answers why. There will be times when it will feel as through the heavens are brass – that your prayers have gone not only unanswered but also unheard. Contrary to what the lies of religion have enticed you to believe, there will be times when the answer is "No." I would ask, respectfully, when it happens, what exactly do you plan to do? What will you do when you don't get your way? Will you see it as a moment of processing, learning to depend even more fully upon the inner voice of the Holy Spirit, or will you, instead, begin to view yourself as a victim, blaming God and questioning yourself?

In times of trial and in moments of testing, it's absolutely vital, absolutely critical even, that your perspective be that of the Kingdom rather than that of the natural, temporal world. As the scriptures remind us, weeping will endure for a night. It doesn't last always. It won't last forever. Yes, it's real. And, yes, it does serve a purpose. However, it doesn't have to last a lifetime. Did you know that you can contribute to your own suffering and heartache simply by choosing to view the process in a self-centered, immature way? It's all too common, really. In fact, within the religion of Christianity, it's unfortunately become the norm.

Suffering and affliction are appointed within the Kingdom of God, but the suffering is only seasonal – it only exists for certain periods of time. And then, as the great pendulum of time passes, morning comes and the darkness fades away, as weeping and mourning turn to laughing and dancing again. There is a season for everything, as the scriptures so eloquently, so brilliantly state. We claim to know that. In times of joy we remember that. However, it seems it's only in the times of suffering that we suddenly become most forgetful of that. In times of affliction we forget that even the suffering exists for a season – and for a reason. My friend and fellow believer, in closing this chapter to you, it is my hope that you will begin to recognize all the more that even your affliction serves a purpose. Through it all, the inner Christ is being revealed within you. You're being refined as gold through the flames of the furnace of affliction and not only will you be better but you will also be brighter in the end.

CHAPTER SIX

THE PURPOSE OF THE PIT

It's no secret, really, that all revelation must be tested. It must be weighed and examined against the scriptures and also against time, in order to be measured. However, what I've come to learn within my own life and within my own ministry is that even the dreams we have will be tested. In fact, even our God-given dreams are forced to endure the flames of renewal and the fires of refinement in order to be more firmly realized and recognized. In my own life, if I were to be completely honest with you, my most powerful dreams were never truly realized without moments of struggle and hardship. Allow me to say here at the very offset of this chapter that if it feels like you're going through a literal Hell on Earth where your dreams and visions are concerned, it's usually a good sign that your dream has come from God.

Nowhere within the entirety of the scriptures is this principle any more revealed than in the account of the life of Joseph – a dreamer, just like you. As you now find yourself reading these words and consuming this revelation of struggle, chances are that in the midst of your turmoil you've forgotten that even your current afflictions serve a purpose within your life. Perhaps, because of pain, you've forgotten to "count it all joy" when you fall. Yet, through it all, something greater is being developed within you and it's slowly beginning to emerge. It's slowly beginning to be brought forth to the surface for all the world to see and to recognize.

Your dream, regardless of how God-inspired it is, will be tested, though. I assure you. And without the testing, you will not fully appreciate the dream you've been given.

The call of God, though it comes without repentance and is never removed or taken away, never comes easily and without cost. The dream you've been given, in fact, will cost you everything within the Kingdom of Heaven, and you will be required to sacrifice all that you have in order to obtain the promise. It was the renowned faith healer Kathryn Kuhlman who when asked about the call of God said, simply, "It will cost you everything. Kathryn Kuhlman died a long time ago." Today, though, in the modern, current Christian religion of "glitz" and "glam," few if any ever talk about the importance of sacrifice. "Everything comes easily if we just believe," we seem to believe.

But is it true? According to the scriptures, the answer is a resounding no.

When Joseph, at a very young age, was given dreams that foretold his God-inspired destiny, not only was he rebuked, mocked, persecuted, and even reviled by his brothers, he was also thrown into a pit. The experience of the pit, though, was only the beginning of his journey into afflictions and from there things seemed to go from bad to much, much worse. After the pit there came the prison. The lies continued. The hate of Joseph continued. He was slandered and maligned. He wasn't believed. He was criticized and his freedom taken away because of the lies of those around him. But then, after he had suffered a while, there came a time in the palace – a time in which he was given not only rule and reign but also the opportunity to help save an entire nation in a time of famine. Suffice it to say, your dreams will always be tested, first, in order to be recognized and then ultimately revealed.

All too often, when believers are given glimpses of their destinies in God, they are shown only the good. They're shown the stage lights, the large bank accounts, the success and the wealth. Most never count the cost. In fact, all too often, most never even truly believe that a cost exists in the first place. After all, Jesus already picked up the tab, right? Without maturity in your faith you will never be able to graduate from the pit to the palace and without recognizing the role the pit plays in the process of God you will never be able to see your dream become a reality. When beginning to write this book, I felt led to include the story of Joseph because it perfectly illustrates the purpose of the "pits" of life. You vision will cost you something – everything in fact. Your ministry for the Kingdom of Heaven will not come easily. And it will not be cheap. You're not only going to be forced to pay a price but you're going to be required to pay full price.

"And Jacob dwelt in the land wherein his father was a stranger, in the land of Canaan. These are the generations of Jacob. Joseph, being seventeen years old, was feeding the flock with his brethren; and the lad was with the sons of Bilhah, and with the sons of Zilpah, his father's wives: and Joseph brought unto his father their evil report. Now Israel loved Joseph more than all his children, because he was the son of his old age: and he made him a coat of many colours. And when his brethren saw that their father loved him more than all his brethren, they hated him, and could not speak peaceably unto him. And Joseph dreamed a dream, and he told it his brethren: and they hated him yet the more. And he said unto them, Hear, I pray you, this dream which I have dreamed: For, behold, we

were binding sheaves in the field, and, lo, my sheaf arose, and also stood upright; and, behold, your sheaves stood round about, and made obeisance to my sheaf. And his brethren said to him, Shalt thou indeed reign over us? or shalt thou indeed have dominion over us? And they hated him yet the more for his dreams, and for his words. And he dreamed yet another dream, and told it his brethren, and said, Behold, I have dreamed a dream more; and, behold, the sun and the moon and the eleven stars made obeisance to me. And he told it to his father, and to his brethren: and his father rebuked him, and said unto him, What is this dream that thou hast dreamed? Shall I and thy mother and thy brethren indeed come to bow down ourselves to thee to the earth? And his brethren envied him; but his father observed the saying. And his brethren went to feed their father's flock in Shechem. And Israel said unto Joseph, Do not thy brethren feed the flock in

Shechem? come, and I will send thee unto them. And he said to him, Here am I. And he said to him, Go, I pray thee, see whether it be well with thy brethren, and well with the flocks; and bring me word again. So he sent him out of the vale of Hebron, and he came to Shechem. And a certain man found him, and, behold, he was wandering in the field: and the man asked him, saying, What seekest thou? And he said, I seek my brethren: tell me, I pray thee, where they feed their flocks. And the man said, They are departed hence; for I heard them say, Let us go to Dothan. And Joseph went after his brethren, and found them in Dothan. And when they saw him afar off, even before he came near unto them, they conspired against him to slay him. And they said one to another, Behold, this dreamer cometh. Come now therefore, and let us slay him, and cast him into some pit, and we will say, Some evil beast hath devoured him: and we shall see what will become of his dreams. And Reuben heard it, and he delivered him out of their hands; and said, Let us not kill him. And Reuben said unto them, Shed no blood, but cast him into this pit that is in the wilderness, and lay no hand upon him; that he might rid him out of their hands, to deliver him to his father again. And it came to pass, when Joseph was come unto his brethren, that they stript Joseph out of his coat, his coat of many colours that was on him; And they took him, and cast him into a pit: and the pit was empty, there was no water in it. And they sat down to eat bread: and they lifted up their eyes and looked, and, behold, a company of Ishmeelites came from Gilead with their camels bearing spicery and balm and myrrh, going to carry it down to Egypt. And Judah said unto his brethren, What profit is it if we slay our brother, and conceal his blood? Come, and let us sell him to the Ishmeelites, and let not our hand be upon him; for he is our brother and our flesh. And his *brethren were content. Then there passed by Midianites merchantmen; and they drew and lifted up Joseph out of the pit, and sold Joseph to the Ishmeelites for twenty pieces of silver: and they brought Joseph into Egypt. And Reuben returned unto the pit; and, behold, Joseph was not in the pit; and he rent his clothes. And he returned unto his brethren, and said, The child is not; and I, whither shall I go? And they took Joseph's coat, and killed a kid of the goats, and dipped the coat in the blood; And they sent the coat of many colours, and they brought it to their father; and said, This have we found: know now whether it be thy son's coat or no. And he knew it, and said, It is my son's coat; an evil beast hath devoured him; Joseph is without doubt rent in pieces. And Jacob rent his clothes, and put sackcloth upon his loins, and mourned for his son many days. And all his sons and all his daughters rose up to comfort him; but he refused to be comforted; and he said, For I will go down into the grave unto my son mourning. Thus his father wept for him. And the Midianites sold him into Egypt unto Potiphar, an officer of Pharaoh's, and captain of the guard." (Genesis 37:1-36 KJV)*

In the midst of pain and suffering it can be so easy to forget your dreams and your visions. In the midst of affliction, when the seemingly unimaginable begins to take place – when you find yourself thrown into the pits of life – it can seem as though the vision and the dream will never come to pass and that the destiny is far-off. Whether you've ever realize it or not, though, your pit serves only to reveal to you your God-given dreams. In fact, the truth of the matter is that your dreams will not fully manifest without time in the pit. Were it not for the pit, Joseph could never have been propelled into his God-given destiny and his dreams could never have come to pass. Without a Judas there could have been no cross and no salvation. In other words, suffice it to say, it's when you're hurt the most that you receive the greatest manifestations of your promises. Keep dreaming. Keep believing. Keep envisioning. I promise you, my friend, you're going somewhere, even in spite of the suffering.

CHAPTER SEVEN

PRESSED

There is a glory within you far greater than that which you can comprehend. There is a treasure within you – buried treasure, in fact. What I've found throughout my own life and continue to see all the more throughout my life in ministry is that most people never take the time to fully understand the greatness existing and residing within them. When Jesus likened the Kingdom of Heaven to buried treasure, hidden within a field, he did so not only to paint a picture of the Kingdom existing within, but he also used the analogy to convey that in order for the treasure to come to the surface and be brought to light a certain amount of uncovering must first take place. You'll never know what exists within you without a certain amount of digging – a certain amount of uncovering. In order to know the greatness existing within you, you're going to have to undergo painful pressing in order for the glory to be revealed.

All throughout the entirety of the scriptures within the New Testament writings, there is reference to an inner, veiled, hidden greatness – a greatness that exists just out of natural sight. It can't be seen with natural, naked eyes. It often goes unnoticed. Most of the time, it can't even be felt, in all honesty. Most of the time, as we go throughout daily life and become so anesthetized in the habits of routine, the sense of greatness seems like nothing more than a dream or fairy tale. But there is greatness existing within you. There always has been, and there always will be, even when you fail to recognize it. What if I were to tell you that in order for your greatness to be revealed to you – and to the world – that you must endure hardship and affliction, first? Would such a concept seem foreign to the religious mind? It usually does. However, we find this principle not only shown through the teachings of Jesus of Nazareth throughout his earthly life and ministry but also within the writings of the Apostle Paul.

Not only did Jesus liken the Kingdom of Heaven to a treasure hidden – buried – in a field, but Paul, also, makes mention of a treasure being placed within "earthen vessels." By doing soul, Paul distinguishes the nature of the inner, hidden Christ from the nature of the human, carnal flesh. A certain sense of distinction is made and a line of demarcation drawn between the natural and the physical.

Suffice it so say that in order for the natural and the physical to be separated, though, requires a certain amount of digging and a certain amount of pressing. You'll never know what exists within you until you're pressed – until you're squeezed. It's truly within the moments of pressing that we find what has always existed within. The Kingdom of God exists entirely upon the premise that what is within you must be revealed outwardly to the world.

"Therefore seeing we have this ministry, as we have received mercy, we faint not; But have renounced the hidden things of dishonesty, not walking in craftiness, nor handling the word of God deceitfully; but by manifestation of the truth commending ourselves to every man's conscience in the sight of God. But if our gospel be hid, it is hid to them that are lost: In whom the god of this world hath blinded the minds of them which believe not, lest the light of

the glorious gospel of Christ, who is the image of God, should shine unto them. For we preach not ourselves, but Christ Jesus the Lord; and ourselves your servants for Jesus' sake. For God, who commanded the light to shine out of darkness, hath shined in our hearts, to give the light of the knowledge of the glory of God in the face of Jesus Christ. But we have this treasure in earthen vessels, that the excellency of the power may be of God, and not of us. We are troubled on every side, yet not distressed; we are perplexed, but not in despair; Persecuted, but not forsaken; cast down, but not destroyed; Always bearing about in the body the dying of the Lord Jesus, that the life also of Jesus might be made manifest in our body. For we which live are always delivered unto death for Jesus' sake, that the life also of Jesus might be made manifest in our mortal flesh. So then death worketh in us, but life in you. We having the same spirit of faith, according as it is written, I believed, and therefore have I spoken; we also believe, and therefore speak; Knowing that he which raised up the Lord Jesus shall raise up us also by Jesus, and shall present us with you. For all things are for your sakes, that the abundant grace might through the thanksgiving of many redound to the glory of God. For which cause we faint not; but though our outward man perish, yet the inward man is renewed day by day. For our light affliction, which is but for a moment, worketh for us a far more exceeding and eternal weight of glory; While we look not at the things which are seen, but at the things which are not seen: for the things which are seen are temporal; but the things which are not seen are eternal." (2 Corinthians 4:1-18 KJV

Notice within the writings of Paul to the church at Corinth the reference to the treasure within – a treasure that is not temporal but is eternal.

And also notice, if you will, the times that Paul speaks of hardship and affliction, noting trouble on every side. Though he references the glory of Christ only briefly, he speaks more so of the pain of affliction and of hardship. Why? Because the glory is never revealed without it. In fact, I would dare to say to you that anyone who tells you that you can have the glory of Christ without also being forced to endure hardship and affliction is lying to you. Do not be deceived. The glory of Christ is revealed to the world – and to you – through moments of trial, moments of testing, moments of affliction, and in moments of adversity.

I would ask you, humbly and respectfully, my friend and fellow believer, what is the glory of Christ truly worth to you? What are you willing to pay? What are you willing to endure? Though the Gospel is freely given, the Gospel itself is not free, nor has it ever been. The

Gospel of Christ will cost you your entire life, just as it did Jesus. And rest assured, contrary to the religious teachings abounding throughout the world today, you and I will be required to pay full price just as Jesus did. The servant is not greater than the master, according to Jesus.

Do you truly believe that you can possess the Kingdom without pain? Do you truly believe that you can go through life without facing moments of apparent loss or setback? Do you think that you can experience resurrection within your life and within your own journey of faith without first being forced to also take the nails of crucifixion? If so, I assure you that you are mistaken. Pressing is one of the many processes of God by which the inner Christ is revealed and uncovered. It's through the pressing that the inner glory is brought forth to the surface for all the world to see. And there is no other way.

Let's examine this in a more natural way, though. What does the pressing look like and what does it feel like in natural life each day? In truth, it feels like "pressure." Chances are you feel it to some extent each and every day of your life. Chances are, also, that you're experiencing it even as you read these words today. When the heat is on and the pressure builds, though, something else is always, always happening just beyond natural sight. While the tension mounts and as we find ourselves being pressed by the trails of life, there is always something taking place deep within – a more hidden, more veiled, more buried, more "hidden" work. And this work is the nature of the inner Christ attempting to be revealed for all the world to see. The inner Christ is being perfected always – even in and especially in moments of pressure.

You are not the life you live within the physical, natural world, as you know. In fact, just as Paul said, there is a very real, very big difference between the temporal and the eternal. The car you drive, the home you live within, and the job you commute to on a daily basis are all temporal. The Christ in you, though, is eternal. You – the real you – will never come to the surface without moments of testing in which the temporal is separated from the eternal. To put it another way, it's only through the act of pressing and only in times of high pressure that the real you can begin to emerge and be brought to the surface. When you feel the pressure, know that you're in the right place within the plan of God. In fact, begin to rethink the "pressures" of life in a new and different way – not through the natural senses but through the eyes of the Holy Spirit instead.

Pressure isn't meant to destroy you, although it may often seem like it or feel like it. No. Instead, pressure is meant to reveal you. It's never meant to kill you; it's meant to bring the real you to the surface. Pressure within the Kingdom of Heaven and within all matters of daily life serves to separate the temporal from the spiritual and the natural from the supernatural. We find this depicted even within the earthly life of Jesus of Nazareth. We find this depicted even within his many, many notable miracles, particularly within the account of the healing of the woman with the issue of blood who touched the hem of Jesus' garment and was made whole. According to the scriptures, she "pressed" through the crowd. Even the miracle you're seeking after within your life will require a certain amount of pressing.

"And a woman having an issue of blood twelve years, which had spent all her living upon physicians, neither could be healed of any, Came behind him, and touched the border of his garment: and immediately her issue of blood stanched. And Jesus said, Who touched me? When all denied, Peter and they that were with him said, Master, the multitude throng thee and press thee, and sayest thou, Who touched me? And Jesus said, Somebody hath touched me: for I perceive that virtue is gone out of me. And when the woman saw that she was not hid, she came trembling, and falling down before him, she declared unto him before all the people for what cause she had touched him, and how she was healed immediately. And he said unto her, Daughter, be of good comfort: thy faith hath made thee whole; go in peace." (Luke 8:43-48 KJV)

The instance is recounted within the Gospel of Mark in this way: *"And a certain woman, which had an issue of blood twelve years, And had suffered many things of many physicians, and had spent all that she had, and was nothing bettered, but rather grew worse, When she had heard of Jesus, came in the press behind, and touched his garment. For she said, If I may touch but his clothes, I shall be whole. And straightway the fountain of her blood was dried up; and she felt in her body that she was healed of that plague. And Jesus, immediately knowing in himself that virtue had gone out of him, turned him about in the press, and said, Who touched my clothes? And his disciples said unto him, Thou seest the multitude thronging thee, and sayest thou, Who touched me? And he looked round about to see her that had done this thing. But the woman fearing and trembling, knowing what was done in her, came and fell down before him, and told him all the truth.*

And he said unto her, Daughter, thy faith hath made thee whole; go in peace, and be whole of thy plague." (Mark 5:25-34 KJV)

Within the account of the miracle in the Gospel of Mark, we find various references to a certain amount of work required on the part of the woman. She had to "press" through the crowd in order to receive her miracle. In fact, according to the text, it was in the "press" that the miracle of healing took place. She wasn't merely an onlooker. She wasn't some bystander, content to sit upon the sidelines. She was determined to receive her miracle, regardless of the "press." Within this passage, we find a very powerful revelation concerning pressure: "Miracles occur under pressure."

If you now find yourself reading these words and feeling pressed or even crushed under the mounting weights of life, rest assured it in no way means that you're outside or apart from the will of God for your life. The pressure, in fact, is a confirmation that your breakthrough is coming. The pressure serves as confirmation of the impending miracle and without the "pressing" there can be no manifestation of your promise within your life. No, it isn't going to be easy, contrary to the lies of religion; however, it's worth it. Yes, there will be work involved. Yes, in order to lay claim to your promise you're going to feel the "pressing," but for a moment I'd like for you to consider the alternative. What happens when there is no pressure? There will remain only more of the same.

In closing this chapter, I want to encourage you, my dear friend and fellow believer, to begin to rethink even the process of "pressure" in a new and different way than ever before. In order for you to begin to see the purpose of the pain, you're going to have to begin to realize that pressure serves to reveal the inner Christ within you. The press brings out what's truly residing within you. Rather than viewing the pressures and the trials of life as attacks from the enemy, begin to view them as processes through which you're becoming more aware of the eternal. It's in the pressing – under pressure – where the natural and the spiritual become separated. And it's there that the Kingdom of Heaven is on full display.

CHAPTER EIGHT

THE 100 FOLD

Blessing is a process. *"But other fell into good ground, and brought forth fruit, some an hundredfold, some sixtyfold, some thirtyfold." (Matthew 13:8 KJV)* It's perhaps one of the most widely misunderstood passages of text within the entirety of the scriptures and a text which, in truth, seems very cryptic at first glance. Within your own personal life and journey of faith I'm sure you've heard this passage of text used in various contexts over the years – often in shocking and even seemingly bizarre ways.

Chances are, too, that you've usually heard this preached in various ministry fundraisers as a way to emphasize the theme of "sowing and reaping." But there's something more – something hidden in plain sight.

It wasn't that long ago that I happened upon a television program late one evening and saw a monthly telethon of a popular religious broadcasting network. The fiery preacher, as he spoke, emphasized the need for viewers to send in their largest contribution, saying that God is bound by His Word to bring about a 100 fold return – that is, only if they called within the next thirty minutes to give their credit card numbers. It's time to grow up in the Kingdom of God. It's time to put away childish things and come to maturity – to mature to perfection. Now, let me say here at the very offset that I'm not sharing this to in any way denounce the fundraising practices of other ministries. No.

Instead, I share this example to illustrate that within the Kingdom of God, we've been deceived into believing that blessing comes easily, with no effort and with no real struggle.

"Just believe," we're told. "If you believe, you'll call the toll-free number on your screen and God will bless you with a 100 fold harvest." What if I were to tell you, though, that the greatest revelation of the text comes not from what Jesus said but rather from what Jesus left unsaid? Would you find that statement shocking? Please allow me to explain. By speaking of a 100 fold return, Jesus was actually alluding to something else – something much more unpopular. I promise you that if you will receive this revelation, never again will you question your Kingdom authority and never again will you ever fall victim to the lies of religion within your life. In the passage of text,

Jesus is speaking emphatically about the Law of Process!

It's one of the most forgotten, most widely understand Universal Laws within Creation and a Law which most wish didn't even exist at all – especially those sincere and well-intentioned believers within Christianity who have been deceived into believing in the quick and easy "fix." It simply cannot be stated enough that within the Kingdom of God and even more so within life itself, there just aren't any easy fixes. Rather than looking for an easy way out, why not begin to mature in Christ and begin to look even deeper into the truth of the scriptures. Jesus wasn't speaking of giving "handouts" to those who believe; he was speaking of enduring a very real, very eternal, often painful "process." In order to better understand this, let us examine for a moment the text in its entirety.

"The same day went Jesus out of the house, and sat by the sea side. And great multitudes were gathered together unto him, so that he went into a ship, and sat; and the whole multitude stood on the shore. And he spake many things unto them in parables, saying, Behold, a sower went forth to sow; And when he sowed, some seeds fell by the way side, and the fowls came and devoured them up: Some fell upon stony places, where they had not much earth: and forthwith they sprung up, because they had no deepness of earth: And when the sun was up, they were scorched; and because they had no root, they withered away. And some fell among thorns; and the thorns sprung up, and choked them: But other fell into good ground, and brought forth fruit, some an hundredfold, some sixtyfold, some thirtyfold. Who hath ears to hear, let him hear. And the disciples came, and said unto him, Why speakest thou unto them in parables? He answered and said unto them, Because it is

given unto you to know the mysteries of the kingdom of heaven, but to them it is not given. For whosoever hath, to him shall be given, and he shall have more abundance: but whosoever hath not, from him shall be taken away even that he hath. Therefore speak I to them in parables: because they seeing see not; and hearing they hear not, neither do they understand. And in them is fulfilled the prophecy of Esaias, which saith, By hearing ye shall hear, and shall not understand; and seeing ye shall see, and shall not perceive: For this people's heart is waxed gross, and their ears are dull of hearing, and their eyes they have closed; lest at any time they should see with their eyes and hear with their ears, and should understand with their heart, and should be converted, and I should heal them. But blessed are your eyes, for they see: and your ears, for they hear. For verily I say unto you, That many prophets and righteous men have desired to see those things which ye see, and have not seen them; and to hear those things which ye hear, and have not heard them. Hear ye therefore the parable of the sower. When any one heareth the word of the kingdom, and understandeth it not, then cometh the wicked one, and catcheth away that which was sown in his heart. This is he which received seed by the way side. But he that received the seed into stony places, the same is he that heareth the word, and anon with joy receiveth it; Yet hath he not root in himself, but dureth for a while: for when tribulation or persecution ariseth because of the word, by and by he is offended. He also that received seed among the thorns is he that heareth the word; and the care of this world, and the deceitfulness of riches, choke the word, and he becometh unfruitful. But he that received seed into the good ground is he that heareth the word, and understandeth it; which also beareth fruit, and bringeth forth, some an hundredfold, some sixty, some thirty. Another parable put he forth unto them, saying, The kingdom of heaven is likened unto a man which sowed good seed in his field: But while men slept, his enemy came and sowed tares among the wheat, and went his way. But when the blade was sprung up, and brought forth fruit, then appeared the tares also. So the servants of the householder came and said unto him, Sir, didst not thou sow good seed in thy field? from whence then hath it tares? He said unto them, An enemy hath done this. The servants said unto him, Wilt thou then that we go and gather them up? But he said, Nay; lest while ye gather up the tares, ye root up also the wheat with them. Let both grow together until the harvest: and in the time of harvest I will say to the reapers, Gather ye together first the tares, and bind them in bundles to burn them: but gather the wheat into my barn. Another parable put he forth unto them, saying, The kingdom of heaven is like to a grain of mustard seed, which a man took, and sowed in his field: Which indeed is the least of all seeds: but when it is grown, it is the greatest among herbs, and becometh a tree, so that the birds of the air come and lodge in the branches thereof. Another parable spake he unto them; The kingdom of heaven is like unto leaven, which a woman took, and hid in three measures of meal, till the whole was leavened. All these things spake Jesus unto the multitude in parables; and without a parable spake he not unto them: That it might be fulfilled which was spoken by the prophet, saying, I will open my mouth in parables; I will utter things which have been kept secret from the foundation of the world. Then Jesus sent the multitude away, and went into the house: and his disciples came unto him, saying, Declare unto us the parable of the tares of the field. He answered and said unto them, He that soweth the good seed is the Son of man; The field is the world; the good seed are the children of the kingdom; but the tares are the children of the wicked one; The enemy that sowed them is the devil; the harvest is the end of the world; and the reapers are the angels. As therefore the tares are gathered and burned in the fire; so shall it be in the end of this world. The Son of man shall send forth his angels, and they shall gather out of his kingdom all things that offend, and them which do iniquity; And shall cast them into a furnace of fire: there shall be wailing and gnashing of teeth. Then shall the righteous shine forth as the sun in the kingdom of their Father. Who hath ears to hear, let him hear. Again, the kingdom of heaven is like unto treasure hid in a field; the which when a man hath found, he hideth, and for joy thereof goeth and selleth all that he hath, and buyeth that field. Again, the kingdom of heaven is like unto a merchant man, seeking goodly pearls: Who, when he had found one pearl of great price, went and sold all that he had, and bought it. Again, the kingdom of heaven is like unto a net,

*that was cast into the sea, and gathered of every
kind: Which, when it was full, they drew to
shore, and sat down, and gathered the good into
vessels, but cast the bad away. So shall it be at
the end of the world: the angels shall come
forth, and sever the wicked from among the just,
And shall cast them into the furnace of fire:
there shall be wailing and gnashing of teeth.
Jesus saith unto them, Have ye understood all
these things? They say unto him, Yea, Lord.
Then said he unto them, Therefore every scribe
which is instructed unto the kingdom of heaven
is like unto a man that is an householder, which
bringeth forth out of his treasure things new and
old. And it came to pass, that when Jesus had
finished these parables, he departed thence.
And when he was come into his own country, he
taught them in their synagogue, insomuch that
they were astonished, and said, Whence hath
this man this wisdom, and these mighty works?
Is not this the carpenter's son? is not his mother*

called Mary? and his brethren, James, and Joses, and Simon, and Judas? And his sisters, are they not all with us? Whence then hath this man all these things? And they were offended in him. But Jesus said unto them, A prophet is not without honour, save in his own country, and in his own house. And he did not many mighty works there because of their unbelief." (Matthew 13:1-58 KJV)

Notice that the text exists within the same context of the inner Kingdom of Heaven. Through parables, Jesus likened the Kingdom to Heaven to certain things, in an attempt to illustrate the existence of an inner, more spiritual, much more eternal reality. Jesus notes that some would receive the teaching and that there would be others who would not – but that the seed would be cast onto the ground equally. To put it another way, no one is exempt from the processes of the Kingdom, whether they like it or not, whether they realize it or not, and, above all, whether they choose to accept it or not. When the seed falls onto good ground, though, different results happen – a greater harvest is brought forth. Suffice it to say that the way in which you choose to view the process of life will directly determine the outcome of your harvest. The way you choose to view the Law of Process within your life will directly be tied to your level of productivity in the Kingdom of Heaven.

But if you're going to move from the realm of thirty to the realm of 60 and then to the realm of 100, you're going to move through the realm of the 40. When I realized this within my own life, it changed the way I view the processes of life, my friend. Oh how I hope and pray the same for you. The number 40 has always, always represented "tribulation" and "trial" and "testing." The scriptures of the Holy Bible are replete with various references to the number 40 as it relates to hardship and struggle and suffering. Jesus was tempted in the wilderness for 40 days. The children of Israel, after the Exodus, were forced to wander through the wilderness for 40 years because of their unbelief. 40 is the number of tribulation, and in order to get to the 100 fold or even to the 60 fold realm within the Kingdom, you're going to have to first pass through the 40 fold realm.

Bear in mind, though, that you were never destined to dwell within the 40 fold realm; you've always, always been destined by God to pass through. Make no mistake, though, there is no blessing without it, and it will be demanded of you that you pass through it. There was no Promised Land without the wilderness. There would have been no power within the life and ministry of Jesus were it not for his time in the wilderness those 40 days. In fact, the scriptures make reference that after being tempted of the devil for 40 days, it was then and only then that Jesus "returned unto Galilee in the power of the Spirit." You will have no promise fulfilled if you do not first begin to pass through the realm of tribulation within your own life. You will be forced to do so. How you do it, though, is entirely your very own choice.

What if the church could begin to recognize that even the times of tribulation serve a very real, very powerful purpose? What if we could, as the collective Body of Christ within the realm of the Earth begin to finally see that it's only in the wilderness that we're made aware of who we truly are? What if we could see that it's only in difficult moments that our true characters are forged in fire and then revealed? You see, not only is the 100 fold realm of God never without price, but the price is indeed a very high price.

The Gospel, though freely given, is never free. The Gospel will cost you your entire life.

No harvest has ever been given simply as a result of one's belief; harvests, according to the scriptures, are given to those who endure till the end. The scriptures make it quite clear that harvests are matters of endurance – even more so than matters of mere believing. We find this truth depicted perhaps best in the Pauline epistles, particularly in Galatians 6:9: *"And let us not be weary in well doing: for in due season we shall reap, if we faint not."* The realm of the 100 fold is reserved not simply for those who believe but, rather, for those who will endure and not faint. But endurance itself can only come through trial and affliction. After all, isn't endurance something that can only come through resistance? If it feels as though all of life is resisting you in this season, do not faint and do not lose heart. Know that the trying of your faith is crafting within you a perfect work. Know that through the resistance you are developing an even greater ability to withstand and to endure.

There is no 100 fold blessing without the 40 fold tribulation. We find reference to this even within the Book of Revelation. As the Apostle John, exiled upon the Isle of Patmos, received the vision, he was shown an immense multitude of people – a number that could not even be numbered. When he asked of their identity, he was told that they were those who had come through tribulation. Within the Kingdom of Heaven, there is no crown without a cost. There is no glory without guts. And there is no true harvest without the act of enduring through times of tribulation. It is only those who overcome – those who come over – who earn the rewards of their faith. If you now find yourself enduring through tribulation, not only are you exactly where you've been ordained, but you are now being prepared for something much greater. Weeping will not last always.

CHAPTER NINE

EVERYBODY HURTS

When I began to feel the inspiration that would come to be this book, I felt within my spirit the immense gravity of what could only be the weight of responsibility. This is not a popular message, and, in truth, the revelation of tribulation is one not widely received. I knew instinctively, though, just how important it was to share this revelation with the world. What I've found within my own life and ministry and continue to see over and over again each day is that when we find ourselves in times of pain and suffering, it can be so easy to feel that we're the only ones who have ever hurt. It simply isn't true, though. The fact of the matter is that everybody hurts.

It isn't some cheap cliché to suggest that everyone hurts and endures pain in life; it's a revelation of life within the Kingdom of God – one that, though unpopular, is vital to understand. As I began to delve deeply into the ancient text of the scriptures, what I began to find was that all throughout the Holy Bible, there are various references of equality – references that, at first glance, may go unnoticed. In life, there truly is a sense of equality where the dynamics of pain and suffering are concerned. The head of the successful business, though he may seem to have it all, is hurting, too. The sincere believer who always seems to have it all together and never seems to have a care in the world is also in pain, though they may never profess to be. The neighbor who has just purchased the new car and who seems to be living the life of luxury puts on a brace face each and every day to face the world, and the world doesn't know that each day he's facing a financial struggle with no apparent end in sight.

Pain is so often hidden behind smiles. In fact, smiles can be very, very deceiving if you truly think about it. They can so easily hide and numb a world of pain; however, smiles never numb the pain. I felt led and inspired to include this chapter within the book because, like so many others, you've chosen to put on a brave face in moments of suffering. You've hidden your pain so very well. To most, it seems that you've kept your faith without question. The truth of the matter, though, if you were to be totally candid with yourself, is that you've been wearing a mask. Chances are, even as you now read these words, you're terrified and have no idea what the future holds. And yet you keep on smiling.

One of the most painful, most inconvenient truths in life is that we're all hurting in some way. It isn't that we aren't all in pain in some way or another; it's simply that some of us are much better at hiding it. According to statistics, as of 2017, major depressive disorder affected approximately 17.3 million American adults, or about 7.1% of the U.S. population age 18 and older, in a given year. 1.9 million children, 3 – 17, have diagnosed depression, according to the CDC, as of the year 2018. The numbers rise each month as more and more individuals – including children – are diagnosed. Shockingly, it's also been found that adults with a depressive disorder or symptoms have a 64 percent greater risk of developing coronary artery disease. What are we to make of this? Are we to simply take away that we, as humans, are doomed to sadness as some necessary evil within the human condition? Most certainly not. According to the scriptures, we are not as those who have no hope.

With the number rising and with more and more diagnoses being made each passing day, within the United States and throughout the world, what do such findings say about the human condition? Are we to simply believe that things are always meant to go from bad to worse as some part of a divine plan and that there's rarely ever, if any, real joy in life? Most certainly not – considering that the joy is our strength, according to the scriptures. Could it be, though, that we've been conditioned religiously to have a very unhealthy view of trial and testing? Think of this for a moment. Could it be that somewhere along the way we've become conditioned to think that life within the

Kingdom will always be easy? Could it be that somewhere along the way, most have believed the religious lie that heartache and suffering are abnormal and should always be fought against? This is to in no way diminish the need to medical supervision where depression is concerned; however it is to say that we as humans can often fight against the very things that, if felt, will provide our own means of escape.

What if rather than fighting against your affliction, you began to see it for what it truly is? What if you began to view the moments of suffering in life as part of the many, many processes of God – tools used to reveal dreams, destinies, and identities within the Kingdom? Could it be that God has never wanted you to fight against your pain but, rather, to recognize its purpose? Imagine such a concept. Could it be, theoretically speaking, that your pain could in fact be greatly diminished by being embraced? Imagine that. For a moment think of what such a concept would mean not only for the world at large but, specifically, for the Body of Christ. What if we truly, truly began to understand that the only way out is, indeed, through? Everything would change.

As I've said and taught for years, the moment you begin to change the way you see your life, your entire life will change. The moment you begin to change the way you see the things around you, those same things will change. Perspective is key – crucial even. But perspective is never any more needed and valuable than when addressing the topic of pain and suffering. Hear me when I say that your outlook of your situation is what is directly determining your situation – and its outcome. What if you could begin to see that your pain and suffering are directly tied to the way that you're choosing to view your pain and suffering? Would such a shift of conscious perspective not also serve to alter the outcome? Most certainly! Jesus himself said that you and I will be given exactly what we believe.

And so I would ask you now, what exactly do you believe about your pain and suffering and your hardship? Do you think that you're the only one? Really? Do you think that you're the only one who's ever lost anyone? Do you think you're the only one concerned about your finances? I assure you that you aren't. Right now, even as you read these words, billions of other people are concerned about their health and wellness. Millions today have received a bad report from their doctors just in the time it's taken you to read this sentence. Right now, somewhere in the world, a child is going to bed hungry after having not eaten in days. Even as you read these words, someone has chosen to end his or her own life because the pain of living seemed almost too overwhelming and the thought of even daring to wake up to another day of pain was too much to bear. So, tell me again why you think you're the only one?

I include this not to seem insensitive to your pain or struggle but to remind you that never ever have you been the only one. We all – myself included – have undergone what at times seemed to be the most horrendous pain and suffering. But, thankfully, we're still here. Thankfully, we've endured. And thankfully, as you well know, it got better after we were made to suffer a little while. We're stronger for it. We're better for it. And whether you realize it yet or not, Christ has been revealed a little more for it. If you look at the theme of pain and suffering throughout the New Testament, you find one resounding theme: "Everybody hurts sometimes."

Interestingly, in the first epistle of the Apostle Peter, we find this theme referenced in a rather remarkable way: *"The elders which are among you I exhort, who am also an elder, and a witness of the sufferings of Christ, and also a partaker of the glory that shall be revealed: Feed the flock of God which is among you, taking the oversight thereof, not by constraint, but willingly; not for filthy lucre, but of a ready mind; Neither as being lords over God's heritage, but being examples to the flock. And when the chief Shepherd shall appear, ye shall receive a crown of glory that fadeth not away. Likewise, ye younger, submit yourselves unto the elder. Yea, all of you be subject one to another, and be clothed with humility: for God resisteth the proud, and giveth grace to the humble. Humble yourselves therefore under the mighty hand of God, that he may exalt you in due time: Casting all your care upon him; for he careth for you. Be sober, be vigilant; because your adversary the devil, as a roaring lion, walketh about, seeking whom he may devour: Whom resist stedfast in the faith, knowing that the same afflictions are accomplished in your brethren that are in the world. But the God of all grace, who hath called us unto his eternal glory by Christ Jesus, after that ye have suffered a while, make you perfect, stablish, strengthen, settle you. To him be glory and dominion for ever and ever. Amen. By Silvanus, a faithful brother unto you, as I suppose, I have written briefly, exhorting, and testifying that this is the true grace of God wherein ye stand. The church that is at Babylon, elected together with you, saluteth you; and so doth Marcus my son. Greet ye one another with a kiss of charity. Peace be with you all that are in Christ Jesus. Amen." (1 Peter 5:1-14 KJV)*

Notice within the text, as the case is made to the early church that suffering serves a purpose, the writer of the passage makes mention of the fact that everyone hurts sometimes. *"Whom resist stedfast in the faith, knowing that the same afflictions are accomplished in your brethren that are in the world." (1 Peter 5:9 KJV)* Personally, I have to admit that I've always found it rather remarkable the way the writer of the text compares the afflictions of the church to the afflictions of those in the world. Notice that though the text is written to the church, the writer makes reference to "brethren that are in the world." There's equality in pain and suffering and hardship. As the scriptures remind us, it rains upon the just as well as the unjust, equally. In other words, you're not the only person experiencing hardship, even though you may believe otherwise.

Although such recognition may not serve to take the pain of struggle away when you've been called to suffer for a while, it's comforting to be reminded that we're not alone. Not only is the Holy Spirit leading and guiding in times of struggle – in times of affliction – but also there are other people just like you who are experiencing many of the same hardships and trials. Should this not make us more empathetic and loving toward others? Should this not make us more compassionate and more hungry to know the stories of others? You just might be surprised to find that those who on the surface seem to be so unlike you actually have a story of suffering similar to your own. Have you allowed the Holy Spirit to make you a little more loving, a little more empathetic, and a little more compassionate through your pain? If not, don't be surprised if you continue to hurt a little longer.

CHAPTER TEN

GREATER GLORIES

It wasn't all that long ago that I found myself in a time of transition within my life and ministry. After having released my fortieth book, the demands upon the ministry seemed to be unending. We were expanding. We were growing as never before. My itinerary had begun to grow to the point that it seemed almost impossible to keep up at times. Throughout the day our offices would receive calls from ministries throughout the world inviting me to minister to their congregations. I'm so thankful for my blessings. I'm so honored to a part of the Kingdom for such a time as this. And, most of all, I'm so very humbled to be a voice to hurting people throughout the world. Your faithful, continued support and your love and prayers continue to make the outreach of this great, prophetic ministry possible.

For me, it was in this time of expansion – this time of growth – that I began to receive the revelations contained within the pages of this book, learning to recognize all the more that with every single blessing and with every gift given, there will also always come a very high demand. In fact, sometimes, it really isn't all that easy to receive blessings. Contrary to what religion has falsely claimed for centuries, every blessing will come with the exchange of a demand. The scriptures are replete with countless examples of this, really. Think about it. There's always an exchange. In the

Kingdom, if you want to receive, you give. If you want to reap, you sow. If you desire healing, you take a step of faith in order to be made whole. And if you truly desire blessing and breakthrough, you exchange what I like to call "sweat equity."

You work. You endure. You persist. You persevere. You continue till the end. And so often, you suffer. It's all part of the process – especially the suffering and the enduring till the end. Ministry isn't easy, and anyone who tells you otherwise either isn't ministering or isn't truly acting on faith. As we've journeyed together through the pages of this book, you've realized that in the Kingdom and within life itself, there are times in which you're going to find yourself pressed and even crushed to the point that you'll sometimes feel you've reached your literal breaking point. What I can share with you from my own life and my own personal ministry, though, is that you'll also be stretched. You'll be forced to expand. You'll be forced to grow. Stagnancy is not tolerated within life, because life is far too precious a gift to ever be wasted by sitting upon the sidelines – particularly the life lived within the Kingdom of God.

The life of faith will demand that your faith be proven and put to the test. In fact, whether you've ever taken the time to realize it yet or not, each and every day, the Universe and all of Heaven and Earth seemingly ask, "Do you truly believe what you say you believe?" Your vision will expand. Your dreams will continue to grow. You'll begin to find many times that the visons of yesteryear no longer seem to fit because you've outgrown them, moving, as Paul said, from "glory" to "glory." This growth – this expansion and never ending journey of faith – implies that to even have faith is to be stretched beyond our own natural limitations. As I've said before, for the mind to be truly renewed and changed, it must first be stretched beyond old paradigms of belief. This growth can often be painful as well.

Sometimes, it hurts to be stretched. It hurts to be moved prophetically through the realm of God into the land of 100 fold returns because there will always be greater demands placed upon your faith when you have endured through tribulation and are prepared to reap your reward. I feel inspired by the Holy Spirit to include this chapter to you because you need to understand that, at times, even blessings won't feel very blissful. There are going to be moments when, just when you think you've arrived, you're going to be forced to move again beyond your comfort zone. You're going to be given a bigger dream. You're going to need to build a larger church. You're going to have to hire more employees. You're going to have to travel more. Although I relate expansion here to terms of ministry, the truth is that expansion ties to all matters of daily life in general, also.

As a prophetic life coach, I have the tremendous honor and joy of speaking into the lives of individuals on a daily basis – other dreamers, just like you. What I've found to be an often consistent theme through the countless millions of prophetic words I've delivered throughout the past twenty-five years, is that because of stretching, even times of great blessing can sometimes feel anything but blissful. Even in times of harvest, you're still going to sweat. You're going to be forced to still endure the heat, as you continue to be a laborer. You'll think of the toil of planting and sowing, thinking of all that's transpired to bring you to where you are, and as you prepare for harvest, you'll still be stretched. The story never really ends.

Throughout more than twenty-five years of prophetic ministry, I've prophesied to heads of business, heads of state, celebrities of the stage and screen, and to millions of individual dreamers just like you, and what I've found to be a consistent theme is that success itself will always demands continued stretching. There are no points of arrival – no points at which you can truly say the work is over. Because with every dream will also come a new dream. With every vision will also come greater insight, greater revelation, and an even greater desire to see more, to do more, to accomplish more, and to be more. The glory you now experience is in no way comparable to the glory that awaits. Hear me when I say to you that there is always, always going to be more to come. And with each new and greater glory will come also great demand and further moments of stretching.

For the dreamer, you see, it isn't enough to simply write one book. It isn't enough to simply begin one successful business. Faith will always demand more. The call of God demands more, requiring that the faith one possesses always be put to the test in order to be stretched. And so I would ask, my friend, while you're growing, what are you doing? While you're reaping the harvest, are you still planting? While you're seeing the fruits of your labor, are you beginning to plant another row of seed to bring about a new and even greater harvest?

I was prophesying to a very popular recording artist once who is a personal client and dear friend. I once asked, "When your album went to number one, how did you feel?" She replied, quite simply, "I was already working on the next album." The same for heads of business and even heads of ministry. When John, the successful head of a popular Fortune 500

Company first came to me to inquire of the Word of the Lord, the vision was clear: "Keep building. Keep growing. Keep expanding" When a friend and fellow author, Tanya, wrote her first bestselling book, the word of the Lord to her was simple, "Begin your next book."

I've included this chapter to you because you need to truly understand that in the journey of faith, there truly are no points of arrival. There truly are no moments at which you can simply be afforded the luxury of sitting upon the sidelines and doing nothing. Even in the off-season, you're going to be demanded to prepare for the next season of harvest. Again, I would ask, while you're busy growing, what are you doing? While you're busy reaping the harvest, what are you doing? Are you preparing for next season? Are you continuing to plant? Are you continuing to build and to dream? If not, then I would argue that you aren't truly putting your faith to the test and using it to its fullest potential.

When Jesus spoke of 100 fold return, he was illustrating the value of the Word as it relates to productivity and potential. The Word will always produce results and, depending upon the condition of the soil, will bring about remarkable results. You've been given a Word within your own life: "There is more to come." The Book of James speaks of faith in a rather extraordinary way that I feel further illustrates this point, speaking of being "doers" of the Word and not hearers only. The writer of the Book of James reminds us that faith will always require action. There truly is no day off.

"James, a servant of God and of the Lord Jesus Christ, to the twelve tribes which are scattered abroad, greeting. My brethren, count it all joy when ye fall into divers temptations; Knowing this, that the trying of your faith worketh

patience. But let patience have her perfect work, that ye may be perfect and entire, wanting nothing. If any of you lack wisdom, let him ask of God, that giveth to all men liberally, and upbraideth not; and it shall be given him. But let him ask in faith, nothing wavering. For he that wavereth is like a wave of the sea driven with the wind and tossed. For let not that man think that he shall receive any thing of the Lord. A double minded man is unstable in all his ways. Let the brother of low degree rejoice in that he is exalted: But the rich, in that he is made low: because as the flower of the grass he shall pass away. For the sun is no sooner risen with a burning heat, but it withereth the grass, and the flower thereof falleth, and the grace of the fashion of it perisheth: so also shall the rich man fade away in his ways. Blessed is the man that endureth temptation: for when he is tried, he shall receive the crown of life, which the Lord hath promised to them that love him. Let no man say when he is tempted, I am tempted of God: for God cannot be tempted with evil, neither tempteth he any man: But every man is tempted, when he is drawn away of his own lust, and enticed. Then when lust hath conceived, it bringeth forth sin: and sin, when it is finished, bringeth forth death. Do not err, my beloved brethren. Every good gift and every perfect gift is from above, and cometh down from the Father of lights, with whom is no variableness, neither shadow of turning. Of his own will begat he us with the word of truth, that we should be a kind of firstfruits of his creatures. Wherefore, my beloved brethren, let every man be swift to hear, slow to speak, slow to wrath: For the wrath of man worketh not the righteousness of God. Wherefore lay apart all filthiness and superfluity of naughtiness, and receive with meekness the engrafted word, which is able to save your souls. But be ye doers of the word, and not hearers only, *deceiving your own selves. For if any be a hearer of the word, and not a doer, he is like unto a man beholding his natural face in a glass: For he beholdeth himself, and goeth his way, and straightway forgetteth what manner of man he was." (James 1:1-24 KJV)*

The Book of James reminds us that faith is always an action word, and without the "acting out" of the dream there is no true faith at work. In closing, you've already accomplished so much and have overcome great adversity. You've already sown so many seeds, often in sorrow and in pain. You have seen the effects of your faith, recognizing the revelation that even suffering serves a purpose and that even in the midst of your pain, you've been given the opportunity to see and to experience greater glories within the realm of the Holy Spirit. It's time now to recognize that you're being stretched for a reason. Your borders are being enlarged for a purpose, and your dream is expanding. As your vision grows, so too will your labor. Yes, the fields are white unto harvest, as the scriptures remind us; however, harvest will come next season, too. While you're growing, while you're planting, and while you're reaping a harvest, continue to do the work. Your faith demands that of you.

CHAPTER ELEVEN

THE JOY OF IT ALL

When I began to receive the revelations contained within this book, being shown glimpses of the purposes of suffering, I have to admit, it didn't feel very good. Such a teaching seems to directly contradict centuries of religious tradition and fly directly in the face of organized religion. We want it easy. Grace is free and all that's required is belief, religion seems to suggest. In moments of hardship, it's the enemy seeking to kill, steal our joy, or destroy what God has destined, we so often think. To begin to say that even pain serves a very powerful purpose and that suffering is part of life in the Kingdom, well, let's face it, it isn't very popular. But it is true. And it does need to be recognized if we as a people are ever going to begin to grow into maturity in the faith.

Joy is strength, according to the scriptures. The joy of the LORD is our strength – the strength which helps us to overcome. But let's face it, it isn't easy to take joy in moments of hardship or struggle. It isn't easy to see the bigger picture, when we find ourselves feeling so forgotten, so abandoned by God, and so alone in the wilderness. Seeing the bigger, grander, more heavenly picture seems almost impossible when suffering arrives. Spirituality ceases to be the central focus whenever pain comes.

Right now, as you read these words and now find yourself in the midst of trial and tribulation, although it may not seem like in this present moment, the truth is that you still have something to look forward to – a lot, in fact. In closing, I wanted to include this chapter to you as a way to offer to you the encouragement of the Kingdom of God – from one overcomer to another. You're still going places. You aren't trapped. You aren't stuck. You aren't lost in the desert, forced to wonder around aimlessly in the heat of the wilderness. Yes, your pain serves a very real purpose within the Kingdom of God; however, so too does your immense, expansive, God-given vision for your life. If you dreams are still intact, there's always hope. And as long as you maintain your vision for a bright future and an expected, anticipated end, absolutely nothing will be able to deter you from your dreams.

Throughout the years, I've spoken and taught often about the "expected end" and need for believers to have a vision for their own bright futures. According to the scriptures, you are not like those who have no hope. The promises and the plans of God have not been recalled. Your gift and calling have not been suspended or terminated simply because it now feels that you're walking through the furnace of affliction. In fact, in the furnace of affliction, the gift and the call of God are made all the more clear – if you can allow yourself to believe it. Right now, although it may not seem like it, your own bright future is still an absolute certainty – just as much as it ever has been. Rather than focusing on the trial of the present moment, I feel inspired by the Holy Spirit to offer you a word of advice – one overcomer to another: "Keep looking forward." Keep persevering. Keep enduring. But, through it all, keep looking forward, setting your eyes upon the God-given dream and destiny now being perfected within you.

When trial and struggle come, it can become so easy to forget all that we've been promised. In moments of heartache and pain, it can all too often seem as though we've been forgotten or neglected. Such is simply not the case, though, I assure you. There are still plans to prosper you. There are still plans to give to you a bright future – one of hope and one of joy. As the scriptures declare, your end will be greater than all your former days, if only you can endure and continue to look forward, remembering always the dream you've been given. What you have sown in tears, you will reap in joy – that is if you faint not.

"They that sow in tears shall reap in joy. He that goeth forth and weepeth, bearing precious seed, shall doubtless come again with rejoicing, bringing his sheaves with him." (Psalm 126:5-6 KJV) As long as you're enduring, you're sowing something. You're planting something.

Rather than sowing bitterness, begin to choose instead to sow hope and optimism, knowing that the trying of your faith is perfecting that faith and that all who have been called to the Kingdom are also called to endure tribulation in life. You haven't been forgotten about. You haven't been neglected. And, above all, you haven't become so lost within the wilderness experience that there's no way back to your land of promise. In fact, it's in this wilderness that, if you will listen more closely, you will hear the gentle whispers of the Holy Spirit reminding you that even this, too, shall pass.

There's still joy to be had. You're going to laugh again. You're going to dance again. You're going to prosper again and dwell within the land of riches and abundance, even though it may not seem like it at this present moment. *"For I reckon that the sufferings of this present time are not worthy to be compared with the glory which shall be revealed in us. For the earnest expectation of the creature waiteth for the manifestation of the sons of God. For the creature was made subject to vanity, not willingly, but by reason of him who hath subjected the same in hope, Because the creature itself also shall be delivered from the bondage of corruption into the glorious liberty of the children of God. For we know that the whole creation groaneth and travaileth in pain together until now. And not only they, but ourselves also, which have the firstfruits of the Spirit, even we ourselves groan within ourselves, waiting for the adoption, to wit, the redemption of our body." (Romans 8:18-23 KJV)*

In this Pauline epistle to the early church at Rome, Paul gives an admonishment to keep looking forward, remembering at all times the prize to come. And in so doing, he also makes a very real, very dramatic comparison, comparing the struggle of the present moment to the joys to come. I've often found this passage of text remarkable. In moments of struggle it can become so easy to forget to look ahead. And yet, within the text, Paul states that a future glory awaits those who can continue to advance in spite of pain and suffering. At first glance such a statement may seem irrelevant – particularly in moments of pain and grief. But a joy still remains for all who will endure and who will maintain their God-given visions.

"Wherefore seeing we also are compassed about with so great a cloud of witnesses, let us lay aside every weight, and the sin which doth so easily beset us, and let us run with patience the race that is set before us, Looking unto Jesus the author and finisher of our faith; who for the joy that was set before him endured the cross, despising the shame, and is set down at the right

hand of the throne of God. For consider him that endured such contradiction of sinners against himself, lest ye be wearied and faint in your minds. Ye have not yet resisted unto blood, striving against sin. And ye have forgotten the exhortation which speaketh unto you as unto children, My son, despise not thou the chastening of the Lord, nor faint when thou art rebuked of him: For whom the Lord loveth he chasteneth, and scourgeth every son whom he receiveth. If ye endure chastening, God dealeth with you as with sons; for what son is he whom the father chasteneth not? But if ye be without chastisement, whereof all are partakers, then are ye bastards, and not sons. Furthermore we have had fathers of our flesh which corrected us, and we gave them reverence: shall we not much rather be in subjection unto the Father of spirits, and live? For they verily for a few days chastened us after their own pleasure; but he for our profit, that we might be partakers of his holiness. Now no chastening for the present seemeth to be joyous, but grievous: nevertheless afterward it yieldeth the peaceable fruit of righteousness unto them which are exercised thereby. Wherefore lift up the hands which hang down, and the feeble knees; And make straight paths for your feet, lest that which is lame be turned out of the way; but let it rather be healed. Follow peace with all men, and holiness, without which no man shall see the Lord: Looking diligently lest any man fail of the grace of God; lest any root of bitterness springing up trouble you, and thereby many be defiled; Lest there be any fornicator, or profane person, as Esau, who for one morsel of meat sold his birthright. For ye know how that afterward, when he would have inherited the blessing, he was rejected: for he found no place of repentance, though he sought it carefully with tears. For ye are not come unto the mount that might be touched, and that burned with fire, nor *unto blackness, and darkness, and tempest, And the sound of a trumpet, and the voice of words; which voice they that heard intreated that the word should not be spoken to them any more: (For they could not endure that which was commanded, And if so much as a beast touch the mountain, it shall be stoned, or thrust through with a dart: And so terrible was the sight, that Moses said, I exceedingly fear and quake:) But ye are come unto mount Sion, and unto the city of the living God, the heavenly Jerusalem, and to an innumerable company of angels, To the general assembly and church of the firstborn, which are written in heaven, and to God the Judge of all, and to the spirits of just men made perfect, And to Jesus the mediator of the new covenant, and to the blood of sprinkling, that speaketh better things than that of Abel. See that ye refuse not him that speaketh. For if they escaped not who refused him that spake on earth, much more shall not we escape, if we turn away from him that speaketh from heaven: Whose voice then shook the earth: but now he hath promised, saying, Yet once more I shake not the earth only, but also heaven. And this word, Yet once more, signifieth the removing of those things that are shaken, as of things that are made, that those things which cannot be shaken may remain. Wherefore we receiving a kingdom which cannot be moved, let us have grace, whereby we may serve God acceptably with reverence and godly fear: For our God is a consuming fire." (Hebrews 12:1-29 KJV)*

Within this passage from the Book of Hebrews, we find what I truly believe to be several keys to remember when enduring affliction – keys that are given as the writer of the text admonishes us to look to Christ. Christ is the author and the finisher of our faith. First, in painting this illustration to the early church, the writer of the text seems to signify that what has a beginning will also have some expected outcome – some finished work. You aren't going to struggle always. You aren't going to always suffer. Even suffering and tribulation have intended outcomes within the Kingdom of God. Secondly, in moments of struggle, remember joy. Remember what joy feels like. Remember what abundance feels like. Bring to remembrance each day all that you've already overcome and were made victorious over. Remember all the times that you did have a smile upon your face – those times long ago before the pain and suffering began. I assure you, my friend, if you can remember the joy, you will find yourself once again beginning to feel that same joy all the more, all over again.

According to the text, it was "for the joy" set before him that Jesus endured the cross, enduring all that he had been destined to endure. Lastly, as he was enduring the process set before him, while maintaining the joy, he had no bitterness in his heart. Pain can all too often serve to calcify our hearts, making us bitter and resentful. The passage from Hebrews speaks of the dangers of planting seeds of bitterness, though. It isn't worth it, regardless of how tempting it may be to become bitter in your times of struggle. It's all too common, really.

You've seen it before, I'm sure, within your own life. At some point you've encountered someone who seems to have no joy – someone so filled with bitterness, resentment, and anger that they seem to dwell in darkness wherever they go. Did you know that bitterness comes from pain and hurt? It's true. In fact, show me someone who seems to be the most bitter, the most vindictive, and the most negative, and I will show you someone who at one point or another felt devastating pain and loss. Although we all hurt and although we all endure pain, not all of us handle it in the same exact ways. Although we all will at times hurt, some of us become bitter and some of us become better. My prayer for you is that regardless of the struggle and tribulation you now find yourself enduring for the glory of Christ, rather than becoming bitter, choose instead to become better.

Although we have absolutely no choice but to endure moments of pain in life, the way that we choose to endure that pain is absolutely a choice. Rather than blaming God or blaming an enemy or blaming other people – or even blaming ourselves – begin to, instead, view the pain as a process. Is a servant greater than his master? No. And so, suffice it to say, if you truly want to see the Christ revealed, like Jesus, you'll also be demanded to in some ways take the nails into your wrists as well. There is no escaping this. Your pain and your suffering within the Kingdom are your cross to bear – yours and yours alone. There can be no escaping it. There can be no denying it. And, above all, there is no easy way out.

My friend, in the Kingdom of God, you will have to go through the fire of refinement in order to come forth as pure gold; however, you don't have to be angry; you don't have to be bitter. What I'm continuing to find within my own walk of faith and continue to see manifested in the lives of believers all throughout the world is that maturity in God is directly linked to the way that you undergo diverse moments of testing. Will you still remember the joy? Will you still hold fast to the God-given dream within you, even when it hurts? Or will you, instead, begin to blame others, blame God, and continue to blame yourself? And therein is the great paradox of faith. We are always being pressed, but we are never truly crushed. Not really. And we can never be defeated.

"Therefore seeing we have this ministry, as we have received mercy, we faint not; But have renounced the hidden things of dishonesty, not walking in craftiness, nor handling the word of God deceitfully; but by manifestation of the truth commending ourselves to every man's conscience in the sight of God. But if our gospel be hid, it is hid to them that are lost: In whom the god of this world hath blinded the minds of them which believe not, lest the light of the glorious gospel of Christ, who is the image of God, should shine unto them. For we preach not ourselves, but Christ Jesus the Lord; and ourselves your servants for Jesus' sake. For God, who commanded the light to shine out of darkness, hath shined in our hearts, to give the light of the knowledge of the glory of God in the face of Jesus Christ. But we have this treasure

in earthen vessels, that the excellency of the power may be of God, and not of us. We are troubled on every side, yet not distressed; we are perplexed, but not in despair; Persecuted, but not forsaken; cast down, but not destroyed; Always bearing about in the body the dying of the Lord Jesus, that the life also of Jesus might be made manifest in our body. For we which live are always delivered unto death for Jesus' sake, that the life also of Jesus might be made manifest in our mortal flesh. So then death worketh in us, but life in you. We having the same spirit of faith, according as it is written, I believed, and therefore have I spoken; we also believe, and therefore speak; Knowing that he which raised up the Lord Jesus shall raise up us also by Jesus, and shall present us with you. For all things are for your sakes, that the abundant grace might through the thanksgiving of many redound to the glory of God. For which cause we faint not; but though our outward man perish, yet the inward man is renewed day by day. For our light affliction, which is but for a moment, worketh for us a far more exceeding and eternal weight of glory; While we look not at the things which are seen, but at the things which are not seen: for the things which are seen are temporal; but the things which are not seen are eternal." (2 Corinthians 4:1-18 KJV)

ABOUT THE AUTHOR

Dr. Jeremy Lopez is Founder and President of Identity Network and Now Is Your Moment. Identity Network is one of the world's leading prophetic resource sites, offering books, teachings, and courses to a global audience. For more than thirty years, Dr. Lopez has been considered a pioneering voice within the field of the prophetic arts and his proven strategies for success coaching are now being implemented by various training institutes and faith groups throughout the world. Dr. Lopez is the author of more than thirty books, including his best-selling books The Universe is at Your Command and Creating with Your Thoughts. Throughout his career, he has spoken prophetically into the lives of heads of business as well as heads of state. He has ministered to Governor Bob Riley of the State of Alabama, Prime Minister Benjamin Netanyahu, and Shimon Peres. Dr. Lopez continues to be a highly-sought conference teacher and host, speaking on the topics of human potential, spirituality, and self-empowerment. Each year, Identity Network receives more than one millions requests from individuals throughout the world seeking his prophetic counsel and insight.

ADDITIONAL WORKS

Prophetic Transformation

The Universe is at Your Command: Vibrating the Creative Side of God

Creating With Your Thoughts

Creating Your Soul Map: Manifesting the Future you with a Vision Board

Creating Your Soul Map: A Visionary Workbook

Abandoned to Divine Destiny

The Law of Attraction: Universal Power of Spirit

Prayer: Think Without Ceasing

Warfare: Stop Attracting It!

And many, many more

Made in the USA
Columbia, SC
31 August 2020

17264197R00124